The Big Book of
Presentation Games

John Newstrom and Ed Scannell are authors of the best-selling McGraw-Hill series, *Games Trainers Play*, including:

GAMES TRAINERS PLAY

MORE GAMES TRAINERS PLAY

STILL MORE GAMES TRAINERS PLAY

EVEN MORE GAMES TRAINERS PLAY

THE COMPLETE GAMES TRAINERS PLAY

THE BIG BOOK OF BUSINESS GAMES

The Big Book of Presentation Games

Wake-Em-Up Tricks, Ice Breakers, & Other Fun Stuff

John W. Newstrom

Edward E. Scannell

McGraw-Hill

New York   San Francisco   Washington, D.C.   Auckland   Bogotá
Caracas   Lisbon   London   Madrid   Mexico City   Milan
Montreal   New Delhi   San Juan   Singapore
Sydney   Tokyo   Toronto

Library of Congress Cataloging-in-Publication Data

Newstrom, John W.
    The big book of presentation games   /   John W. Newstrom and Edward
E. Scannell.
      p.   cm. — (The big book of business games series)
    ISBN 0-07-046501-0 (paper)
    1. Business presentations. 2. Group games. I. Scannell, Edward
E. II. Title III. Series.
  HF5718.22.N49 1997
  658.4'5—dc21

                                                                 97-35043
                                                                     CIP

McGraw-Hill

A Division of The **McGraw·Hill** *Companies*

        4 5 6 7 8 9 0 DOC/DOC 9 0 0 9

ISBN 0-07-046501-0 (pbk.)

*The sponsoring editor for this book was Richard Narramore, the editing
supervisor was Fred Dahl, and the production supervisor was Pamela
Pelton. It was set in Frugal Sans by Inkwell Publishing Services.*

Printed and bound by R.R. Donnelley & Sons, Inc.

McGraw-Hill books are available at special quantity discounts to use as premiums and sales promotions, or for use in corporate training programs. For more information, please write to the Director of Special Sales, McGraw-Hill, 11 West 19th Street, New York, NY 10011. Or contact your local bookstore.

 This book is printed on recycled, acid-free paper containing a minimum of 50% recycled de-inked fiber.

Contents

Acknowledgments

Any project like this is always a team effort. There is no way we could possibly thank the thousands of "team members" who have continually encouraged and assisted us in our continuing quest to make meetings more effective.

To the thousands of friends and colleagues who have attended our seminars and workshops for such groups as the American Society for Training and Development, Meeting Professionals, Int'l., and the National Speakers Association, we are most grateful. They have helped us field-test the items in this book and have contributed to many of its ideas.

For the continuining assistance from the McGraw-Hill team of Philip Ruppel and Richard Narramore, we are truly indebted. They have become friends as well as our publishing team.

Thank you!

INTRODUCTION

GAMES FOR PRESENTATIONS

Admittedly, you may already be questioning our premise—"games?" In these days of re-engineering, retooling, downsizing, rightsizing (capsizing!), or whatever term may be "in," how can one even think of such frivolity as games in the workplace? Games? Games for businesspeople? You've got to be kidding! Believe us—we're not kidding at all. As a matter of fact, we're serious about this business, and we are in total agreement that the world of "business" is indeed serious. So whether you're the CEO, the sales manager, the team leader, or anyone else who occasionally has the responsibility of making a presentation–either for your organization or for your own department or team—then this book is clearly for you!

GIVING PRESENTATIONS

The purpose of this section is to identify some types of presentations, and then offer several concrete, usable ideas that will make your next presentation more effective.

Types of Presentations

Since we're using the term "presentations" in its most generic sense, let's categorize talks into the following areas:

1. *To inform:* Is your purpose to "tell and sell"? Many training or educational programs fall into this category since they may be providing cognitive information for new skills, knowledge, or attitudes. It may take the form of an address at the weekly Rotary or Kiwanis Club, or it may be the CEO addressing several hundred people at a company's introduction of new software. Whatever the venue or group, the main purpose of this type of presentation is to bring forth information. To further underscore the importance of this objective, Marvin Cetron, a well-known futurist, reports that upwards of 85% of all new information is brought forth in meetings.

2. *To motivate or persuade:* We can certainly agree with the premise that all motivation is internal. Nevertheless, it's always good to get our "batteries recharged," as is so often done at the large motivational rallies across the globe. Often, a lineup of well-known celebrity speakers "do their thing" in trying to get their audiences inspired to go on to "bigger and better" things. While these types of presentations have a place in the marketplace, all too often the results are short-term. Within a week or two, the typical attendee is right back in the same old groove. Nonetheless, these types of presentations are important.

3. *To get action:* This type of presentation can take the form of a hotel sales manager working with association executives or meeting planners to "sell" them on using a particular hotel for their upcoming conference or annual convention. It might be as brief as two people addressing a specific problem and getting closure and action, or it could be a person selling an entire buying team or committee.

4. *To solve problems:* This could be a group or team effort that gets together to attack a single problem. Perhaps conflict resolution is the goal. Typically, this type of presentation is heavily interactive and the speaker takes on the role of a facilitator.

Note: This brief listing, of course, is not meant to be exhaustive. No clear-cut lines, for example, distinguish or differentiate one type of presentation from another.

USING GAMES IN PRESENTATIONS

Interactive exercises or games have been used to liven up presentations ever since it was discovered that people have a very short attention span! If you doubt that, how much can you remember of what a speaker said last week at that luncheon meeting? More to the point, can you recall two or three of the points that a salesperson told you this morning? In fact, some recent studies claim that the span of attention for most of us varies anywhere from ten seconds to three or four minutes! It's easy to see, then, why people become easily bored (or overwhelmed) and respond much better when a talk has life and variety.

CHARACTERISTICS OF GAMES

Let's take a look at some of the characteristics of activities, games, and other types of involvement techniques, and show how they can be used in almost any of your presentations. Games usually:

1. *Are quick to use:* They can range from a five- or ten-second physical activity to a one-minute visual illustration or verbal vignette. However, since the activity should be used to add to or supplement the main purpose or content of the meeting, the time devoted to the game should be minimal.

2. *Are inexpensive:* In general, nothing has to be purchased, nor does an outside facilitator or consultant have to be engaged. With few exceptions, the games included in this book can be used at little—if any—cost.

3. *Are participative:* To be used effectively, the games should involve the participants physically (through movement) or pyschologically (through visual or mental activity, thought, or action). Games typically help people focus their attention, and make them think, react, speak, and, most importantly, even have fun learning!

4. *Are low-risk:* All the games in this book have been field tested dozens of times in many settings with various audiences. When matched to the proper content, the right context, the right people, the right climate, and when used in a positive manner, they will always work for you. The games are user-friendly, and people respond to them in that same positive manner.

5. *Are adaptable:* The best activities, just like the best humorous stories, can be adapted to fit almost any situation, and help reinforce the points you want to make in your talk. They can be modified slightly and still retain their original flavor and character. In fact, it is highly recommended that you tailor the game as much as possible to fit your goal.

6. *Are single-focus:* Games are best used when they demonstrate or illustrate just one major point. As such, they are oriented to micro issues rather than macro issues. Keep them simple and focused, and they will do their job for you!

1

Session Openers and Speaker Introductions

PARTICIPANT PICTURES

OBJECTIVE

To help the presenter and participants learn the names of group members.

MATERIALS REQUIRED

An instant-developing camera and film.

PROCEDURE

Using a quick-developing camera, take registrants' pictures at the time they first register for the program. This is most useful in those extended sessions (3- or 5-day) where participants attend a get-acquainted social session on the previous evening.

Write the name of the individual in the margin or on the reverse side of the picture.

The entire set of pictures can then be reviewed prior to the first work session. This allows the presenter to gain name—face familiarity with group members much more rapidly than otherwise possible. It is particularly useful in those settings (e.g., with side-arm chairs) where the use of tent cards for names is impractical.

ALTERNATIVES

1. Affix the entire set of pictures on a large poster board. Include participant names and relevant data (e.g., company unit or job/title) beside each. Place the display near the entry door or at the refreshment table where group members can conveniently study it.

2. Hire a local caricature artist to create humorous interpretations of each group member (and the presenters) before the first session and post them conspicuously. Since these often capture a significant facial or personality characteristic, they can be equally useful for facilitating the memorization of names and faces. They can also be distributed at the end of the last session as a special "graduation" gift.

SOURCE

Various, including Gordon Inskeep (Arizona State University) and Mark Hammer and Leroy Johnson (Washington State University).

EXPECTATIONS

OBJECTIVE

To help ensure that the stated objectives of the presentation are in general concert with those of the participants.

MATERIALS REQUIRED

Form on page 7.
Handout with session objectives and key topics.

PROCEDURE

At the beginning of the session, distribute a handout describing the session objectives and key points. Then state the objectives and present an overview of the session with the major points and subpoints of the session.

Tell the attendees to review the handout with objectives and key topics and check or circle their primary objective in attending this session so that you can make sure their individual objectives are "in sync" with those objectives already stated. (If the attendees were given an advance agenda of the topics, most of their expectations will likely fall into these already identified areas.) If participants have objectives that have not been mentioned, ask them to jot down their objectives.

If there are fewer than 15 people in the group, after participants individually identify their primary objectives, ask each person to state the objective.

If there are more than 15 people, read each objective and ask for a show of hands to indicate how many people have that objective as their primary objective.

Then ask if there are other objectives that have not been addressed. On occasion, a participant's need may surface that is outside the objectives or content of the program. If so, thank the individual or group for stating the need, but suggest that this particular topic is really outside the agenda. If the requested topic is one with which you have some experience, offer to spend time with the individual(s) at break times to discuss it. If it is outside your area of expertise, ask the group if they can assist. In all likelihood, a colleague will happily respond.

IF YOU HAVE MORE TIME

Tell the attendees that in order to make sure their individual objectives are "in sync" with those objectives already stated, they will be asked to jot down two or three items they are looking for in this session. (They should use "Expectations" form copied from page 7.)

After participants individually write down their own expectations, form groups of three or four people to compare and report on expectations.

After groups report their findings, these are summarized and recorded on flip charts. As individual or group responses are reported, acknowledge each and every item.

Allow 15–20 minutes for this version of the exercise.

EXPECTATIONS

7

THROW AWAY YOUR TROUBLES

OBJECTIVE

To enable participants to get several responses to an individual problem or concern.

MATERIALS REQUIRED

Paper, pencils, empty boxes or containers.

PROCEDURE

This exercise can be used at almost any time during a training session. For programs over a half-day in length, this activity can be used intermittently during the course. Announce that participants will now have a chance to "throw away" their problems. Have each person think of a question, problem, or concern about the topic being addressed. (If a participant cannot think of a relevant item, any problem is okay.) After participants write out their anonymous particular problems, ask them to crumple up the papers and throw them in a container (a box or receptacle that will be placed in the center of the room). For larger groups, have several containers around the room. Be sure not to use regular waste baskets unless they are empty!

After all papers are in the receptacles, ask any person to pick out a crumpled paper and toss it to anyone in the room. Whoever catches it opens the paper and reads the problem aloud. A three-person team is formed (the receiver and one person on each side). The team is given a "30-second timeout" to discuss possible solutions or answers. During this time, the rest of the group is asked to jot down two or three answers or responses.

The team gives its responses, followed by others in the group who can assist.

Repeat the process as time permits.

APPROXIMATE TIME REQUIRED

Minimum 4–5 minutes; expanded as time allows.

I'M GLAD I'M HERE

OBJECTIVE

To start the training program with a positive and humorous opening.

PROCEDURE

Immediately after the introduction, tell the group that you're glad to be there also! To prove that, go around the room asking, "If you weren't here today, what would you be doing that you're glad you don't have to do?" Keep the answers light and fast-moving.

APPROXIMATE TIME REQUIRED

10 minutes.

SOURCE

Sue Hotchkiss, City of Phoenix, Phoenix, AZ.

BUT I'VE ALWAYS DONE IT THAT WAY...

OBJECTIVES

To illustrate how easy it is to develop and continue using unconscious habits.

To point out that there are often equally effective, alternative ways to accomplish an objective.

To illustrate that old ways of doing things may interfere with our acquisition of new behaviors, and therefore require "un-learning" first.

PROCEDURE

Ask one or more participants (e.g., all those wearing a suit coat, sports jacket, or even a windbreaker or cardigan sweater) to stand and remove their coats. As them to put the coats on, noting which arm goes in first. Next, ask them to take the coats off again, and put them on this time by putting the other arm in first.

DISCUSSION QUESTIONS

1. How did it feel to reverse your normal pattern of donning your jacket? (How did it look to observers who were watching?)

2. Why was it so tough (awkward) to do?

3. What prevents us from adopting new ways of doing things? How can we make changes without old habits interfering with them?

4. How can we open ourselves to change within the program, and accept the fact that there may be equally effective (or better) ways to accomplish our tasks than we've used before?

APPROXIMATE TIME REQUIRED

5–10 minutes.

SOURCE

Bob Holmes, Mt. Olive, AL.

MYTHOLOGIZING (CONSTRUCTING OR REACTING TO MYTHS)

OBJECTIVE

To dramatically illustrate to a group that it is easy for them to hold mistaken perceptions about the topic of interest.

PROCEDURE

Define "myth" for participants—"a fiction or half-truth that appeals to the consciousness of people while expressing some of their deep, commonly felt emotions."

Progressively disclose to them some common myths in our society today, such as:

a. One size fits all.

b. You're only as old as you feel.

c. The check is in the mail.

d. Money is the root of all evil.

e. I'm from the government, and I'm here to help you.

f. It'll only take a minute to fix this.

g. There's nothing really wrong with you.

h. There is no discrimination in this organization.

i. Everybody is doing it his or her way.

Then add one or more myths pertinent to the topic of the current training session, such as:

a. Once a customer sees our new product, it will sell itself.

b. Our new procedure for doing this is much easier (or simpler, faster, cheaper) than before.

Then proceed to focus on the myth by asking the questions listed below.

DISCUSSION QUESTIONS

1. Where might this myth have come from?
2. What factors contribute to its perpetuation?
3. What can we do to dispel this myth?
4. Is it indeed a myth, or is there a large measure of truth to it?

APPROXIMATE TIME REQUIRED

A few minutes to introduce the myths; then the myth theme can be woven through the remainder of your presentation.

GUEST SPEAKER INTRODUCTION

OBJECTIVE

To introduce a guest speaker (VIP, etc.) in a novel way.

MATERIALS REQUIRED

Guest speaker or trainer's bio.

PROCEDURE

Secure a copy of the guest speaker or trainer's bio or introduction. Actually cut up the sheet and distribute pieces to several participants in advance so each has a sentence or two to read or memorize.

When you bring up the guest speaker, state: "Our guest is such a celebrity, I'll bet you know more about [him/her] than I do." Then, on cue, the participants relate something about the speaker's background.

APPROXIMATE TIME REQUIRED

2–3 minutes.

THE STANDING OVATION

OBJECTIVE

To provide a bit of levity at the beginning of a program.

PROCEDURE

Walk into the room in which the participants are assembled. Invite everyone to stand up and spread out (approximately an arm's length apart).

Tell them that to make sure they are awake and receptive to the material in your session, you will lead them in an exercise designed to help get their blood moving more rapidly and stimulate the nerve endings in their hands.

Direct them to stretch their arms out at their sides (horizontally from their bodies). When they have all done so properly, then ask them to rapidly bring their hands together, then back to their sides (repeating the two-step sequence about ten times in rapid succession).

Conclude by telling the group that you aren't sure how much better they feel now, but that you feel really good, because this is the first time in all your years of presenting that you have begun a session to a standing ovation!

2

Icebreakers and Participant Introductions

GETTING ACQUAINTED I

OBJECTIVES

To enable participants to become acquainted.

To help build a climate of friendliness and informality.

MATERIALS REQUIRED

Blank stick-on name tags.

PROCEDURE

Each person is given a blank name tag and asked to put his or her first name or nickname on it. Then they are asked to list two words or brief phrases that tell something about themselves that can be used as conversation starters. Examples could be home states, hobbies, children, etc. An illustration follows:

Elizabeth (Beth)

1. Arizona resident

2. Jogger

After giving the group enough time (about 1 minute) to write down their two items, have them start mixing around in groups of two or three (maximum). Every few minutes, tell the group to "change partners" in order to encourage everyone to meet as many new people as possible.

DISCUSSION QUESTIONS

1. Was this exercise helpful to you in getting to know some other people?

2. What kinds of items made the greatest impact on you?

3. How do you now feel about your involvement in this group?

Ask participants to list five words or brief phrases that tell something about themselves that can be used as conversation starters.

After giving the group enough time (about 5 minutes) to write down the five items, have them start mixing around in groups of two or three (maximum). Every few minutes, tell the group to "change partners" in order to encourage everyone to meet as many new people as possible.

TIP

To speed up the activity, give participants a blank name tag when they check in for the program and ask them to write their names, nicknames, and list of descriptive words on the name tags at that time.

GETTING ACQUAINTED II

OBJECTIVE

To allow participants to become acquainted through a structured exercise.

MATERIALS REQUIRED

Blank name tags.

PROCEDURE

At the opening session of a group meeting, each individual is given a blank name tag. Each person completes the following items:

1. My name is _____.

2. I have a question about _____

_____.

3. I can answer a question about _____

_____.

Give participants a few minutes to respond to the statements, then allow 5 minutes in which the group is encouraged to meet and mix with as many people as possible.

TIPS

To speed up the activity, give participants a blank name tag when they check in for the program and ask them to write the requested information on the name tag at that time.

Preprint the name tags with items 1 through 3 above, and ask participants to complete the information as they register or as they wait for the session to begin.

THE MYSTERY PERSON

OBJECTIVE

To encourage newcomers and "oldtimers" to make new acquaintances and get them to mix with other participants.

MATERIALS REQUIRED

Cash prizes.

PROCEDURE

At larger conferences or meetings, the new attendee is often left alone and may have difficulty in getting acquainted. Established cliques are hard to crack and the first-time attendee may feel completely *apart from* rather than *a part of* the group.

To encourage all participants to be more friendly with everyone, designate (in advance and secretly) someone as Mr. or Ms. Mystery Person. Prior to and during the first few sessions, promote the exercise by publicizing, "Shake hands with the Mystery Person. He (she) will give you $1." (Or, "Every tenth person gets $5," etc.)

Properly publicized, this exercise can be both fun and rewarding. It is especially useful for breaking the ice and creating a warm and friendly atmosphere.

DISCUSSION QUESTIONS

1. Why are we reluctant to meet new people? (Each new encounter is a challenge to "sell" ourselves and learn about others.)

2. What was the impact of a possible cash incentive on your behavior? (Met more people; talked with them only superficially.)

3. What are some useful conversation-openers that can help us overcome our reticence?

BINGO GAME

OBJECTIVE

To subtly force newcomers to make new acquaintances in a nonthreatening climate.

MATERIALS REQUIRED

Bingo cards (one for each person).

PROCEDURE

Using prepared bingo-type cards or sheets (see form on page 31), people are asked to move around the room until they find a person who fits the description shown. That person then signs his or her name in the appropriate slot.

Tell participants they have 5 minutes to collect signatures.

BINGO GAME

DIRECTIONS: *Each blank space identifies something about the people in this _____ (seminar, meeting, session, etc.). Seek out your fellow participants and if one of the listed items pertains to them, ask them to sign their names in the appropriate place on your Bingo card. (Even though more than one item may be relevant to any person, only one blank spot should be signed.)*

BINGO

PLAYS TENNIS	IS WEARING RED	PLAYS SOCCER	CHAPTER OFFICER	HAS GRANDCHILDREN
_____	_____	_____	_____	_____
DRIVES A SPORTS CAR	HATES FOOTBALL	LOVES FOOTBALL	FLIES A PLANE	SPEAKS FOREIGN LANGUAGE
_____	_____	_____	_____	_____
PLAYS PIANO	HAS TROPICAL FISH	FREE	SKIS	COMMITTEE CHAIRPERSON
_____	_____		_____	_____
HAS RED HAIR	HATES SPINACH	HAS TWO CHILDREN	LIKES CAMPING	HAS ATTENDED NATIONAL CONFERENCE
_____	_____	_____	_____	_____
FIRST TIME ATTENDEE	DRIVES PICKUP	BROWN EYES	READS *NEWSWEEK*	VISITED FOREIGN COUNTRY
_____	_____	_____	_____	_____

INTRODUCTION BY ASSOCIATION

OBJECTIVE

To aid participants in recalling each others' names.

PROCEDURE

Tell participants that they will be asked to introduce themselves to the group by standing up, stating their names, and associating their names with some item they would bring with them on a picnic (or other activity). Examples:

"My name is Mable, and I'd bring a table."

"My name is Dan, and I'd drive a van."

"My name is Fred, and I'd bring the bread."

"My name is Walt, and I'd bring the salt."

"My name is Kay, and I'd bring the insect spray."

ALTERNATIVE PROCEDURE

You can ask each group member to select a personal characteristic that helps identify himself or herself, and do so by rhyme or alliteration, such as:

"I'm Jovial Joe."

"I'm Sue, with eyes of blue."

DISCUSSION QUESTION

How can the principle of association be used to help participants learn (remember) other (more important) elements of technical knowledge in our program? (General answer: By providing them with old concepts they can associate new ones with, or by stimulating participants to identify their own relevant associations for the new ideas.)

WHO ARE YOU?

OBJECTIVE

To enable participants to become acquainted with one another in an informal setting.

MATERIALS REQUIRED

Paper and pencils or pens for all participants.

PROCEDURE

Individuals are instructed to jot down one question that they would like to ask a person whom they are just meeting. Suggest they be creative and not ask the more obvious questions (name, organization, etc.).

After allowing 1 minute, ask the participants to start moving around, exchanging questions and answers. Encourage the group to meet as many new people as possible in the next 3 minutes.

Call time and ask participants to return to their seats.

DISCUSSION QUESTIONS

1. What were some of the more interesting things discovered about people? Would they have been uncovered in "normal" cocktail party conversations? Why not?
2. What were some of the more productive questions asked?
3. What questions proved to be less productive? Why?

Have participants jot down three questions that they would like to ask a person whom they are just meeting. Suggest they be creative and not ask the more obvious questions (name, organization, etc.).

After allowing 3–5 minutes, ask the participants to start moving around, exchanging questions and answers. Encourage the group to meet as many new people as possible.

Reassemble the entire group and have all persons introduce themselves. As each individual is introduced, other participants are encouraged to add other pieces of information or details shared earlier. This will eventually provide a highly enriched composite picture of each participant.

Allow about 20–30 minutes for this version of the exercise.

NAME TAG MIXER

OBJECTIVE

To help participants get acquainted.

MATERIALS REQUIRED

Name tags.

PROCEDURE

As each participant enters the meeting room, check off his or her name on the roster, but present a different person's name tag. Explain that they should seek one another out, and also introduce themselves to other participants as well.

IF YOU HAVE MORE TIME

If the group is relatively small (up to 30 or 35 participants), have the paired individuals interview each other so they can introduce their counterparts to the rest of the group.

WHAT'S YOUR SIGN?

OBJECTIVE

To help participants get acquainted.

MATERIALS REQUIRED

Signs or charts with each astrological sign and the corresponding dates.

PROCEDURE

Post the signs or charts with each astrological sign around the room, far enough apart to allow a group to gather near each sign and hold a discussion without being overly disruptive to the other 11 groups.

At the beginning of a session, have participants physically move to the part of the room where their sign is located. When groups are formed, allow them 5 minutes to introduce themselves and discuss some of the traits readily associated with their respective signs. (If you are working with a large group, limit the subgroups to five or six participants.)

Call time when 5 minutes have elapsed and ask participants to return to their seats.

If time permits, ask a few groups to report their findings.

DISCUSSION QUESTIONS

1. Are the traits and characteristics of your sign valid ones?
2. Do we sometimes let our "signs" influence our behavior? Why or why not?
3. Have you seen cases when one's astrological sign has been helpful (or obstructive) in work relationships?
4. Do your own self-perceptions "fit" your sign?

HANDFUL OF ICEBREAKERS

OBJECTIVE

To help participants become acquainted with and feel comfortable about each other early in a session.

MATERIALS REQUIRED

Soft ball (for #4).

PROCEDURE

1. Pair up the participants. Instruct pairs to interview each other on the basis of one or more of the following, depending on the time available:

    a. Three unusual things that have happened in their lives.

    b. Special talents or hobbies they have.

    c. The two most important job responsibilities they have.

    d. The person that they most admire (or despise) in the world.

    e. A color and an animal that best describe who they are and how they feel.

2. Ask participants to introduce themselves as they think their best friends would—their likes and dislikes, recreational interests, personal aspirations, etc.

3. Ask participants to introduce themselves with the following instructions: "Tell us your full name, any nickname or abbreviation, who you were named after, and whether you like or dislike your name. Also, tell us what other name you would choose if you had the opportunity, and why."

4. Procure a soft ball (tennis ball or sponge-construction ball). Arrange the participants in a circle. Throw the ball

to one person and ask that individual to disclose something unusual about himself or herself. Then have the ball thrown to another and repeat the process. Only upon the second receipt of the ball should participants disclose their first names.

TREASURE HUNT

OBJECTIVE

To allow a small group (15–25 attendees) at a meeting, presentation, or
program to get acquainted.

MATERIALS REQUIRED

Treasure Hunt handout forms and a nominal prize.

PROCEDURE

At the start of the program, explain the importance of becoming acquainted with the other participants. Hand out
copies of the form on page 45 to each attendee and ask that
everyone find at least one similarity (e.g., "grew up in Chicago") and one dissimilar trait (e.g., "football fanatic" vs. "dislike sports") for at least two other participants. Tell participants they have 4 minutes to complete the assignment.

IF YOU HAVE MORE TIME

Instruct participants to find one similar and one dissimilar
trait for between eight and ten other participants. Explain
that the first person finished should let you know because
she or he will win a prize. Allow 15–20 minutes.

SOURCE

Gordon Hills, St. Petersburg, FL.

TREASURE HUNT

Name _____

INSTRUCTIONS: *Circulate around the room finding one trait you have in common (e.g., "newcomer to city") and one item quite dissimilar (e.g., "has worked for same organization over ten years" vs. "third job this year!") for as many other participants as you can.*

NAME	ALIKE	DIFFERENT
1. _____	_____	_____
2. _____	_____	_____
3. _____	_____	_____
4. _____	_____	_____
5. _____	_____	_____
6. _____	_____	_____
7. _____	_____	_____
8. _____	_____	_____
9. _____	_____	_____
10. _____	_____	_____

THE WHOLE ROOM HANDSHAKE

OBJECTIVE

To have participants meet at least half of the entire group.

PROCEDURE

Have the group form into two large circles—one inside the other. Participants in the inner circle turn and face those in the outer ring, quickly introduce themselves, and continually move to the right. The outer circle rotates left and the inner circle rotates right until all participants meet each other. (Note: This activity works best with groups of 100 or fewer.)

SOURCE

Maggie Bedrosian, The Synergy Group, Silver Spring, MD.

Attention-Getters

WHAT KIND OF EMPLOYEE ARE YOU?

OBJECTIVE

To encourage new employees to make advance decisions about the type of person they intend to become inside the organization.

MATERIALS REQUIRED

Three glasses, two aspirin tablets, two Bromo Seltzer tablets, two Alka Seltzer tablets, and a towel for clean-up.

PROCEDURE

Fill three glasses about three-quarters full of water and place them on a table in view of all participants. Place two aspirin in the first glass. Suggest that the lack of any overt response is analogous to a "do-nothing" employee.

Place two Bromo Seltzer tablets in the second glass. Note that this type of employee has a great burst of initial enthusiasm, but quickly loses it.

Place two Alka Seltzer tablets in the third glass. Note that this type of employee produces a relatively strong but stable output (and hence is the most desirable).

ALTERNATIVE PROCEDURE

Explain that there are three types of employees in the workforce today. The first type **makes** things happen; the second type **watches** what happens; and the third type **wonders** what happened! This story is especially effective if illustrated with Retrophane transparency film, in which the first key word (makes) can be written on the overhead with permanent ink, while the second and third key words (watches and wonders) should be written with their disappearing-ink pen. The point can then be vividly demonstrated that only those who **make** things happen will survive over the long term.

APPROXIMATE TIME REQUIRED

5 minutes.

SOURCE

Glen T. Presley, Blue Cross/Blue Shield, Chicago, IL.

HOW OBSERVANT ARE WE?

OBJECTIVE

To demonstrate that people are often not very observant about ordinary things.

MATERIALS REQUIRED

A nondigital watch.

PROCEDURE

Ask someone in the group if you may borrow his or her watch for a moment. (*Caution:* Make certain it is a nondigital type.) Tell that person (after the watch's receipt) that you would like to test his or her powers of observation, and ask the entire group to silently "play along" with the individual whose watch you are using. Tell the individual to assume that the watch was lost and you found it. Before you return it, you want to make certain the watch can be identified by its owner. Some sample questions include: "What's the brand name?" "What color is the face?" "Anything else printed on the face?" "Roman or Arabic numerals?" "All 12?" "Does the watch have the date and/or day on it?" "Second hand?"

If the group is silently responding as the volunteer attempts to vocally answer the questions, the point is more easily made (i.e., most people cannot totally and accurately describe their own timepieces even if they look at them dozens of times a day).

DISCUSSION QUESTIONS

1. Besides me, who else flunked this test? Why?

2. Why aren't we more observant? (Time pressure, lack of concern, taking things for granted, etc.)

3. Have you seen incidents when people have overlooked commonplace things and problems have resulted?

APPROXIMATE TIME REQUIRED

5 minutes.

ESP ICEBREAKER

OBJECTIVE

To attract and focus the group's attention on you and the presentation to follow.

MATERIALS REQUIRED

Chalkboard or flip chart and chalk or marker; prepared large display card.

PROCEDURE

Ask for a volunteer to assist you. Explain that you are going to foretell the results of an arithmetic exercise by the virtue of ESP, extra-sensory perception. Position yourself any place where you *cannot* see what the person is going to write. Ask the volunteer to write on the flip chart or chalkboard any three-digit number. (*Note:* The number must *not* be a mirror image, e.g., 323.) Then tell the person to reverse the number and subtract the lower number from the higher one. For example:

$$\begin{array}{r} 821 \\ -128 \\ \hline \end{array}$$

Now reverse this number and add it to the preceding product to obtain:

$$\begin{array}{r} +693 \\ \underline{396} \\ 1089 \end{array}$$

As the volunteer completes the calculation, hold up a prepared display card on which you had previously written the number 1089.

Note: This exercise will *always* result in the number 1089. On occasion, the initial subtraction will yield a two-digit number. For example:

$$786$$
$$\underline{-687}$$
$$99$$

In such a case, simply direct the volunteer to add a zero in front (99 changes to 099). Proceed as indicated earlier:

	099	
Reverse it to	+990	and the
resulting sum again is:	1089	

FIVE EASY QUESTIONS

1. What is your favorite color?
2. Name a piece of furniture.
3. Name a flower.
4. Pick a number from one to four.
5. Name an animal in a zoo.

OBJECTIVE

To demonstrate that (some) behavior is quite predictable.

PROCEDURE

Give each participant a sheet of paper and a pen or pencil. Tell them that they will be asked to name five items *very* quickly in response to five questions. It is their *first* reaction that is desired. Then *quickly* ask them:

1. What is your favorite color?
2. Name a piece of furniture.
3. Name a flower.
4. Pick a number from one to four.
5. Name an animal in a zoo.

Then display the following answers: red, chair, rose, three, lion.

DISCUSSION QUESTIONS

1. How many had each item "correct"? (Ask for a show of hands. A surprising number will have chosen these responses.)
2. What does this illustrate to you? (Some human behavior, attitudes, or reactions are predictable. The key is to be an alert observer. A humorous illustration is contained in the story of the person who noted that one-half of all high school seniors scored below average on a certain test!)

SOURCE

Eden Ryl, Ramic Productions, Newport Beach, CA.

THE NATIONAL SALES REPRESENTATIVES' TEST

OBJECTIVE

To allow participants to humorously self-assess their expertise in their profession or line of work.

PROCEDURE

In a light way, tell the group you are going to administer the National Sales Representatives' Test. (*Note:* The title and questions can be easily changed to fit the particular group.)

Have participants place their right hands on a flat surface with fingers outstretched, except that the knuckles on the second (middle) fingers stay tightly on the flat surface.

Advise the group that you are going to ask four simple questions. If the answer is "Yes," they are to respond by raising the thumb or finger you indicate.

1. "Start with your thumb. Are you involved in sales? If yes, raise your right thumb high."

2. "Okay, thumb down. Now for the 'pinkie.' Do you have an interesting job? If so, raise the smallest finger."

3. "Now for the forefinger or index finger. Do you enjoy what you're doing? If so, raise your forefinger."

4. "Thank you. Now with thumb and fingers in their original positions, here's the last question. Using the *ring finger*, and please be honest with us, are you really any good at your job? If you are, raise your ring finger."

The quick laughter will indicate that if participants hold their knuckles and other fingers down, it is practically impossible to raise their ring fingers.

APPROXIMATE TIME REQUIRED

5 minutes.

MIND OVER MATTER

OBJECTIVE

To demonstrate that the power of the mind is such that mental suggestions can actually cause physical movement.

PROCEDURE

Ask participants to clasp their hands together with the two forefingers extended parallel at a distance of one to two inches, as illustrated below.

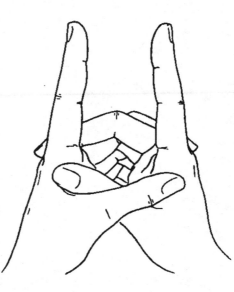

Tell them to study their forefingers and imagine there is a tight rubber band around them. Now state in a deliberate tone and in a slow speed, "You can feel that rubber band bringing your fingers closer … and closer … and closer… ." The smiles and laughter of at least half your audience will tell you they are getting the message, and their fingers are closing together. Experience indicates that half to two-thirds of a group will respond accordingly.

DISCUSSION QUESTIONS

1. What prompted your fingers to move?

2. Have you observed other incidents when mental suggestions have prompted action?

3. For those whose fingers remained motionless, what were you doing to counteract the "rubber band"?

HOW GOOD IS 99.9%?

OBJECTIVE

To help participants think about the impact of mind-sets like "That's good enough for me," or "The customer doesn't expect any more than that."

MATERIALS REQUIRED

Optional: Duplicate "If 99.9% Is Good Enough, Then ..." handout on page 65, and distribute it after you have surprised your audience with the information contained in it.

PROCEDURE

Ask participants what quality level, expressed as a percentage of total items produced, they would accept if they were placed in charge of a product line or service. Poll them, by a show of hands, as to the level acceptable to them. For example:

Level	# Responses
90	
95	
96	
97	
98	
99	

Then indicate that some contemporary firms have sought to hold their reject rates down to just 1/10th of 1 percent (99.9% quality)! Ask them if they think 99.9% quality is adequate.

Next, illustrate some of the effects of even a 99.9% quality level by progressively revealing the startling statistics on page 65.

Finally, you might inform them of Motorola's commitment to achieve "Six Sigma" quality levels—fewer than three rejects per million items produced!!!

DISCUSSION QUESTIONS

1. Would *you* still be satisfied with 99.9% quality?

2. Should our *customers* be satisfied with that level?

IF 99.9% IS GOOD ENOUGH, THEN...

12 newborns will be given to the wrong parents daily.

114,500 mismatched pairs of shoes will be shipped each year.

18,322 pieces of mail will be mishandled every hour.

2,000,000 documents will be lost by the IRS this year.

2.5 million books will be shipped with the wrong covers.

2 planes landing at Chicago's O'Hare airport will be unsafe every day.

315 entries in *Webster's Dictionary* will be misspelled.

20,000 incorrect drug prescriptions will be written this year.

880,000 credit cards in circulation will turn out to have incorrect cardholder information on their magnetic strips.

103,260 income tax returns will be processed incorrectly during the year.

5.5 million cases of soft drinks produced will be flat.

291 pacemaker operations will be performed incorrectly.

3,056 copies of tomorrow's *Wall Street Journal* will be missing one of the three sections.

4

Meaningful Stories About Life

THE ZEN KOAN (A CUP OF TEA)

OBJECTIVE

To open participants' minds to possibilities of new learning.

MATERIALS (OPTIONAL)

Cup, saucer, coffee (or tea or water), and a tray to catch the overflow.

PROCEDURE

At the beginning of a presentation, relate the following tale to the participants. It is a Zen Buddhist Koan—a centuries-old, meaningful story about life.

<u>A</u>
<u>Cu</u>
<u>p</u>
<u>of</u>
<u>Te</u>
<u>a</u>

Nan-in, a Japanese master, received a university professor who came to inquire about Zen. They chatted a while. Nan-in then served tea. He poured his visitor's cup full, and then kept pouring. The professor watched the overflow until he could no longer restrain himself. "It is overfull. No more will go in," he exclaimed.

"Like this cup," Nan-in said, "you are full of your own judgments, opinions, and speculations. How can I show you Zen until you empty your first cup?"

ALTERNATIVES

1. Wait to tell the story until a participant emerges as a "know-it-all" who has heard it all before, and then use it as a parable for the entire group. (This requires great skill, and may risk offending at least one person.)

2. Instead of telling the story by narration, arrange the props listed and have an accomplice (another presenter or a participant) help you in role-playing the vignette. If presented properly, the additional realism can have great impact on the participants.

DISCUSSION QUESTIONS

1. How does this relate to our presentation?

2. Who has experienced being the Zen master? The student? How did it feel?

3. What basic concepts are being emphasized in this role?

SOURCE

Reps, P., *Zen Flesh, Zen Bones* (New York: Anchor, 1961), p. 27.

THE PIKE (HOT STOVE) SYNDROME

OBJECTIVE

To show participants that the limits to their use of the program material lie within themselves as much as externally.

PROCEDURE

Relate the story of the northern pike, placed in one-half of a large aquarium, with numerous minnows unavailable to it in the other half of the glass-divided tank. The hungry pike makes numerous efforts to obtain the minnows, but only succeeds in battering itself against the glass, finally learning that reaching the minnows is an impossible task. The glass plate partition is then removed, but the pike does not attack the minnows. The same pattern of behavior can be viewed in a cat that jumps onto a hot stove (once!). The subsequent behavior of the pike and cat demonstrate the Pike Syndrome, characterized by:

1. Ignoring differences,
2. Assumption of complete knowledge,
3. Overgeneralized reactions,
4. Rigid commitment to the past,
5. Refusal to consider alternatives,
6. Inability to function under stress.

DISCUSSION QUESTIONS

1. What are some examples when people you know have exhibited the Pike Syndrome?

2. How can we help others (or ourselves) break out of the Pike Syndrome?

3. In what ways is the Pike Syndrome useful?

SOURCE

Eden Ryl, Ramic Productions' film, *Grab Hold of Today*.

TALE OF THE PROCESSIONARY CATERPILLARS

OBJECTIVE

To stimulate trainees to be aware of the dangers of passively accepting what others say and do.

PROCEDURE

Share this tale with the group: There is a type of caterpillar called a processionary caterpillar, so named because one will establish a direction and all the others will fall in very closely behind and move in the same path. As a matter of fact, the followers' behavior becomes so automatic that their eyes become half-closed as they shut out the world around them and let the leader do all the thinking and decision making about which direction to pursue. Their behavior is rote and automatic.

An experiment by the French naturalist Jean-Henri Fabre demonstrated the rigidity of the processionary caterpillars' behavior when he enticed the leader to start circling the edge of a large flower pot. The other caterpillars followed suit in a tight procession, forming a closed circle in which the distinctions between leader and follower became totally blurred, and the path had no beginning and no ending. Instead of soon getting bored with the nonproductive activity, the caterpillars kept up their mindless search for several days and nights until they dropped off the edge through exhaustion and starvation from lack of food. Relying totally on instinct, past experience, custom, and tradition, the caterpillars achieved nothing because they mistook activity for achievement.

DISCUSSION QUESTIONS:

1. In what ways are employees like processionary caterpillars?
2. Are trainees like yourselves susceptible to falling prey to the phenomenon of processionary caterpillars? Explain.

3. How can we prevent ourselves and others from becoming like the caterpillars in this story?

APPROXIMATE TIME REQUIRED

5 minutes.

SOURCE

H. Kent Baker and Ronald H. Gorman, Washington, D.C.

RESISTANCE TO CHANGE

OBJECTIVE

To demonstrate to participants that they need to confront their own resistance to change before they can achieve the greatest benefit from a training experience.

MATERIALS REQUIRED

Overhead transparency of Dvorak keyboard, if desired.

PROCEDURE

Tell the group to assume that you have developed a new product that has tremendous potential organizational benefits. A good example is the Dvorak Simplified Keyboard for typewriters and word processors, which allegedly had the potential to increase operator efficiency by over 40 percent; see illustration on page 77.

Ask the group to list all the positive reasons why people should discontinue using the old "QWERTY" keyboards and adapt the new Dvorak system.

Now ask the group to predict all the reasons why people will resist using the new keyboard. Then ask them to categorize those reasons as primarily rational (e.g., too costly, too bulky, wrong size) or primarily emotional (e.g., "I'd have to learn something new.").

Now tell them that you plan to introduce them to some new ideas in this training program that have the potential to improve their personal and organizational effectiveness.

a. Ask them to predict why they and others will resist embracing the new ideas or methods. Which of these factors are rational, and which are emotional?

b. Ask them to list the positive reasons why they should be open to the new ideas or methods you will discuss.

DISCUSSION QUESTIONS

1. Why do we tend to think that other people (but not us) resist change?

2. What can we do to better facilitate change in other people?

3. What can I do in this program to make it more likely that you will accept the changes I offer to you?

4. What will you commit yourselves to do to make yourselves more open to the changes you will hear about?

APPROXIMATE TIME REQUIRED

15–20 minutes.

SOURCE

Adapted from Tom Reilly, Ellisville, MO.

DVORAK SIMPLIFIED KEYBOARD

7   5   3   1   9   0   2   4   6   8   = +

: ;   , '   P   Y   F   G   C   R   L   & /   — 22%

A   O   E   U   I   D   H   T   N   S   - _   — 70%

: ;   Q   J   K   X   B   M   W   V   Z   — 8%

Shift

Shift

space bar

77

THE DUMB JOKE

OBJECTIVE

To encourage participants to ask (dumb) questions.

PROCEDURE

Relate the following story to the group (with a straight face).

"Have you heard the one about the graduate student who was doing a study? He had a cockroach and he set it on a table and told the cockroach to jump. And it jumped to the end of the table. The student picked the cockroach up and pulled off a couple of legs. Then he set it back down and told it to jump. The cockroach jumped about halfway down the table. The student picked it up and pulled off a couple more legs and set it down. He then told the cockroach to jump and it just jumped a little way. Then the student picked it up and pulled off the cockroach's last two legs and set it down. He told the cockroach to jump and it didn't move. So the student concluded that a cockroach with no legs is deaf."

Told properly, the joke will (at best) obtain groans from your audience.

DISCUSSION QUESTIONS

1. "Why would I tell a dumb joke like that?" (To loosen up the audience.)
2. "What lessons are there for you in that incident?" (No one should be afraid to make a "dumb" statement or ask a "stupid" question.)

SOURCE

Cal Green, Telxon Corporation, Houston, TX.

5

Audience Brainteasers

WIN, PLACE, SHOW, OR WHAT?

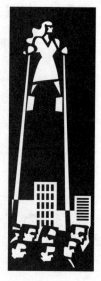

OBJECTIVES

To illustrate the importance of being a top finisher (e.g., 1, 2, or 3).

To provide participants with an opportunity to demonstrate the breadth of their knowledge in a lighthearted fashion.

To introduce a review of four key ideas from your presentation.

MATERIALS REQUIRED

Transparency of the quiz on page 85, or reproduced handouts of the quiz.

PROCEDURE

Select as many of the questions on page 85 as time allows and create an overhead transparency or duplicate handouts for participants.

Set the stage by illustrating how important it apparently is in society to be competitive. For example, in most athletic events only the first-, second-, and third-place finishers receive significant recognition. In industry, it is important to be a leader—in product design, in delivery, in service, in cost, in quality, etc. (GE's CEO, Jack Welch, demanded that all business segments be either #1 or #2 in their markets.) In short, we rarely remember the fourth-place finishers.

But *the fourth item is often critically important.* And the mind can capably handle about four substantial items. Demonstrate, by giving the quiz on page 85 (either individually or in small groups). Then let the group score themselves when you solicit the correct answers from them, or provide them to the group.

DISCUSSION QUESTIONS

1. How do you feel about your memory?
2. Did groups do better than individuals? Why?
3. What are four key things you will never forget about *this* training program?

SOURCE

Sydney Harris.

WIN, PLACE, SHOW, OR WHAT?
(THE MISSING FOURTHS QUIZ)

HANDOUT

1. The four largest cities in the world are Mexico City, Tokyo/Yokohama, São Paolo, and _____ ?

2. The "four freedoms" pronounced by President F. D. Roosevelt were Fear, Want, Speech, and _____ ?

3. The next number in this arithmetic series is 2, 3, 5, ___ ?

4. Becoming prime minister in 1940, Winston Churchill told the British people that he could promise to bring them only "blood, toil, tears, and _____ ?"

5. Area measurements are given in square inches, feet, yards, and _____ ?

6. The 4-H club members make pledges to Head, Heart, Hands, and _____ ?

7. The books of the Bible begin with Genesis, Exodus, Leviticus, and _____ ?

8. The first four presidents of the U.S. were George Washington, John Adams, Thomas Jefferson, and _____ ?

9. The Greek alphabet begins with the letters alpha, beta, gamma, and _____ ?

10. The largest lakes in the world are the Caspian Sea (Asia-Europe), Lake Superior (U.S.), Lake Victoria (Africa), and _____ ?

THE MISSING FOURTHS: KEY

1. City—Seoul

2. Freedom—Worship

3. Number—7

4. Churchill's promise—Sweat

5. Area—Rods

6. 4-H pledge—Health

7. Bible book—Numbers

8. President—Madison (or Thomas Jefferson, if you count his second term)

9. Greek letter—Delta

10. Lake—Aral Sea

THE NINE DOTS

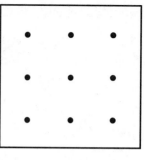

OBJECTIVE

To suggest to participants that their preexisting mind-sets might constrain their capacity to learn new ideas.

KEY

To force one's mind to expand beyond the self-imposed "box" created by the nine dots.

MATERIALS REQUIRED

A means of displaying the nine dots and the solution; paper and pencils or pens for all participants.

PROCEDURE

Display to the group the following configuration of nine dots. Ask them to reproduce the dots on a sheet of paper. Assign them the task of connecting all nine dots by drawing four straight, continuous lines (without lifting their pencils or retracing a line). Allow them a few minutes to make several attempts. Ask how many solved the task successfully. Then either ask a volunteer to step forward and display the correct solution, or else show them the key (found on page 91) on an overhead transparency projector.

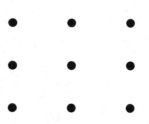

ALTERNATIVE SOLUTIONS

1. The task can also be solved with three straight continuous lines. The first starts at the top of the upper left dot, extends through the center of the upper middle dot, on through the bottom of the upper right dot, and out beyond that dot. The second line returns through the second set of three dots, descending gradually from right to left. The last line returns through the bottom three dots.

2. Another approach is to fold the paper so the three lines of dots align closely. Then a single (wide) pencil line will touch all nine dots simultaneously.

3. A third approach is to take a paint brush and, with a single sweep, connect all nine dots simultaneously.

DISCUSSION QUESTIONS

1. What is the impact in our minds of the configuration of the nine dots? (We mentally create a square and try to circumscribe it with the four lines, leaving the center dot untouched.)

2. What is the key to solving the puzzle? (Getting out of the boxes that we, or others, create for ourselves.)

3. What implications does this exercise have for this program or meeting and for our jobs?

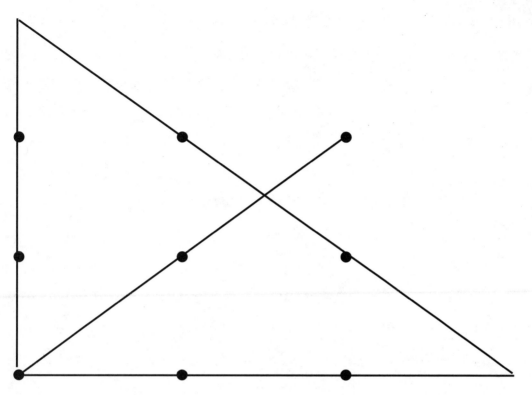

A COUPLE BOUGHT A HOUSE

OBJECTIVE

To get participants to factor a problem into its proper components and relationships.

KEY

Participants must develop a rational arithmetic system for tracing the profit or loss. It can be done by adding the two proceeds and subtracting the two investments. The danger is to use some of the numbers more than once.

MATERIALS REQUIRED

A preprinted description of the incident.

PROCEDURE

Participants are provided with a written description of the following incident.

"A couple bought a house for $160,000. Soon thereafter, they sold it for $170,000, upon moving out of town. A few months later, they were transferred back to town and purchased the same house for $180,000. Then they grew tired of the house and resold it for $190,000."

Question: How much money did the couple gain or lose (or break even) on the exchange?

Then poll the group to determine the frequency with which each of the following answers was obtained.

Gained $20,000

Gained $10,000

Broke even

Lost $10,000

Lost $20,000

IF YOU HAVE MORE TIME

First ask the participants to solve the problem individually. Then break them into small groups of three to five persons to resolve the problem on a collective basis (reaching total consensus).

DISCUSSION QUESTIONS

1. What factors prevent us from solving the problem correctly?

2. Why were the groups able to solve the problem with greater accuracy?

3. What lessons does this hold for approaching similar problems?

TIP

The correct answer is $20,000.

SOURCE

Adapted from N.R.F. Maier and A.R. Solem, "The Contribution of a Discussion Leader to the Quality of Group Thinking: The Effective Use of Minority Opinions," *Human Relations,* 1952, 5, pp. 277–288.

EQUATION QUIZ

$$E = mc^2$$

OBJECTIVE

To exercise participants' minds at the start of a session, or to help them "shift gears" to a different topic.

MATERIALS REQUIRED

Copies of the handout on page 97.

PROCEDURE

Distribute copies of the handout. Each item represents an equation, acronym, or well-known phrase.

EQUATION QUIZ

1. 1 = R.A. in E.B.

2. 10 = L.I.

3. 3 = L.K. that L.T.M.

4. 4 = S. on a V.

5. 5 = T. on a C. (including S. in T.)

6. 6 = P. on a P.T.

7. 7 = Y. of B.L. for B. a M.

8. 2 = G. of V.

9. 9 = J. of the S.C.

10. 10 = D. in a T.N. (including the A.C.)

11. 76 = T. that L. the B.P.

12. 20 = C. in a P.

13. 3 = S.Y.O. at the O.B.G.

14. 66 = B. of the B. (in the K.J.V.)

15. 15 = M. on a D.M.C.

16. 20 = Q. (A., V., or M.)

17. 7 = D. with S.W.

18. 30 = S. over T.

19. 8 = D. a W. (in the B.S.)

20. 2,000 = P. in a T.

ANSWERS: EQUATION QUIZ

HANDOUT

1. 1 = Rotten Apple in Every Barrel

2. 10 = Little Indians

3. 3 = Little Kittens that Lost Their Mittens

4. 4 = Strings on a Violin

5. 5 = Tires on a Car (including the Spare in the Trunk)

6. 6 = Pockets on a Pool Table

7. 7 = Years of Bad Luck for Breaking a Mirror

8. 2 = Gentlemen of Verona

9. 9 = Justices of the Supreme Court

10. 10 = Digits in a Telephone Number (including the Area Code)

11. 76 = Trombones that Led the Big Parade

12. 20 = Cigarettes in a Pack

13. 3 = Strikes You're Out at the Old Ball Game

14. 66 = Books of the Bible (in the King James Version)

15. 15 = Men on a Dead Man's Chest

16. 20 = Questions (Animal, Vegetable, or Mineral)

17. 7 = Dwarfs with Snow White

18. 30 = Seconds over Tokyo

19. 8 = Days a Week (in the Beatles' Song)

20. 2,000 = Pounds in a Ton

HIDDEN SQUARES

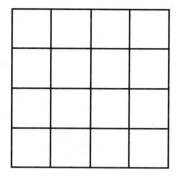

OBJECTIVES

To encourage participants to dig deeper into problems, and visualize them from a different perspective.

To encourage participants to see not only the whole, but also various combinations of parts.

MATERIALS REQUIRED

A flip chart, transparency, or handout with the figure found on page 103.

PROCEDURE

Participants are provided with a visual drawing of a large square divided into smaller squares. They are then directed to quickly count the total number of squares seen, and report that number orally.

KEY

The correct answer is 30, developed as follows: 1 whole square, 16 individual squares, 9 squares of four units each, and 4 squares of nine units each.

DISCUSSION QUESTIONS

1. What factors prevent us from easily obtaining the correct answer? (We stop at the first answer. We work too fast.)
2. How is this task like other problems we often face? (Many parts comprise the whole.)
3. What can we learn from this illustration that can be applied to other problems?

HIDDEN SQUARES FIGURE

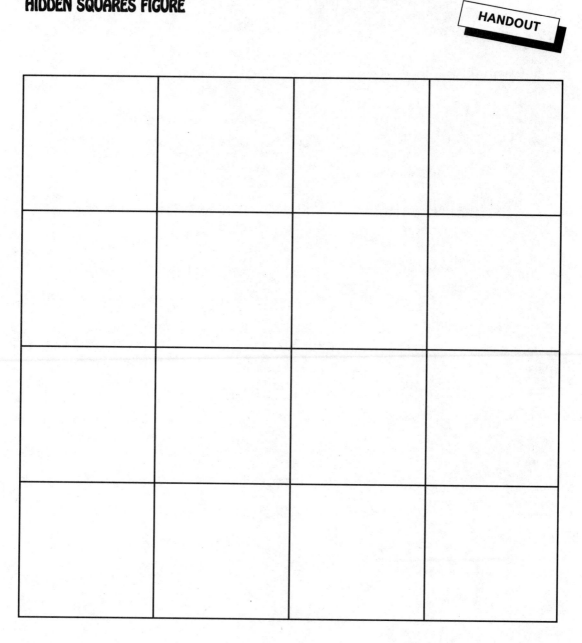

6

Creating Discussion Groups

MIXING IT UP

$$\boxed{N \div X}$$

OBJECTIVE

To create discussion groups of different composition, with a minimum of confusion, delay, or hard feelings.

MATERIALS REQUIRED

Name tags, tent cards, or Ping-Pong balls.

PROCEDURE

1. A classic procedure is to simply announce to the group that you would like them to break into discussion groups of five persons each (for example), and give them a discussion topic or task assignment and the time to complete it.

2. Another approach, especially useful where precision is important in getting the same number of people into each group, is to have the audience "count off." To determine the repetitive number to use for this purpose:

   a. Count the number of people in total (=N).

   b. Determine the number of people that you want to be in each group (=X).

   c. Divide N by X and have the group count off from one up to that number and repeat across the group until everyone has a number.

   d. Instruct participants to locate themselves at a table with all other persons of that number.

3. Another method is to preassign a number or letter to each person by writing it on their name tag or tent card. Then, when you wish to break them into new groups, simply request all A's to join together, all B's, all C's, etc.

4. A fourth procedure is to prepare in advance a set of numbered Ping-Pong balls (with the desired allotment of 1's, 2's, 3's, etc.). Then simply announce your desire that they form into groups. Begin to throw out the balls to the participants, until everyone has caught (or retrieved) one. Then direct them to find others with the same number and form into discussion groups.

SOURCE

Pifter Jagers, Management Center "DeBaak," Noordwyk, Holland.

MIX OR MATCH

OBJECTIVES

To provide a series of options for expeditiously creating newly mixed groups during a presentation.

To preplan the process of creating different sized groups.

MATERIALS REQUIRED

Name cards or tent cards; advance worksheet.

PROCEDURE

Determine how many participants you will have in the session.

Assess how many different mixtures of participants you will need throughout the session, and how many persons you want in each subgroup.

List the participants on a worksheet similar to the example on page 111. Then progressively assign a number, letter, symbol, color, product name, or other differentiating characteristic to each member. Note that you can create varying numbers of groups and varying subgroup sizes in this fashion.

When creating tags or tent cards, simply code them with this information (e.g., Maria Santiago #3, B, yellow, Toasted Granola Flakes.)

Whenever you need to establish new task-oriented or discussion groups, simply instruct all the "yellows" (blues, reds, etc.) to get together. Next time, instruct all the circles to join together, etc.

Note: If you fail to prepare enough preplanned mixtures and need a newly mixed group, simply ask them to form new groups that have no two symbols alike (e.g., a square, circle, triangle, and arrow all in the same group).

SOURCE

John Newstrom, Duluth, MN.

MIX OR MATCH WORKSHEET (SAMPLE)

Name	#	Letter	Symbol	Color	Other
Anna	1	E	Square	Blue	
Bob	2	A	Circle	Red	
Carole	3	B	Triangle	Yellow	
Duffy	4	C	Arrow	Blue	
Elaine	5	D	Square	Red	
Fosdick	6	E	Circle	Yellow	
Greg	1	A	Triangle	Blue	
Heidi	2	B	Arrow	Red	
Ida	3	C	Square	Yellow	
Jorge	4	D	Circle	Blue	
Keith	5	E	Triangle	Red	
Lori	6	A	Arrow	Yellow	
Maria	1	B	Square	Blue	
Nils	2	C	Circle	Red	
Opal	3	D	Triangle	Yellow	
Pete	4	E	Arrow	Blue	
Quincy	5	A	Square	Red	
Roxy	6	B	Circle	Yellow	

THE "66" TECHNIQUE

OBJECTIVE

To get a large group actively involved in a discussion session.

MATERIALS REQUIRED

A room with movable chairs or table and chair setting; flip charts and markers; masking tape.

PROCEDURE

The "66" discussion technique allows for small groups to discuss any type of relevant or pertinent topic. It is a variation of any typical small-group discussion method. It is more structured in that the total group is divided into six-person teams. Have each group identify a recorder. (Note that all groups could have different or similar topics.) After a problem is assigned to each of the groups, a 6-minute period of time is allowed for the group to talk about the issue. Tell the group when there are 2 minutes left; then, with 1 minute left, suggest that the group use the last minute to wrap things up. Depending on the time available, get representative reports from as many groups as possible.

Time spent is contingent upon the size of the group and time restraints. Allow between 10 and 15 minutes to form groups, hold the discussion, and obtain some group reports.

IF YOU HAVE MORE TIME

Have each group post its report on flip chart paper and physically attach it to the wall with masking tape. Call on a representative of each group for a report.

DISCUSSION QUESTIONS

1. What did your group conclude?
2. How do the reports from the various groups compare or contrast?
3. What effect did the time limit have on your group's capacity to generate a meaningful set of responses?

SOURCE

J. Donald Phillips, "Report on Discussion 66," *Adult Education Journal,* 1948, 7, pp. 181–182.

BRAINSTORMING

OBJECTIVE

To give participants an opportunity to engage in a creative problem-solving exercise.

MATERIALS REQUIRED

A paper clip for display at each table.

PROCEDURE

Research indicates that creativity can be cultivated by the use of simple and practical exercises. All too often, however, the spark of innovative thinking is dampened by killer phrases like, "We tried it last year," "We've always done it that way," and a host of similar comments.

To acclimate participants by flicking on their innate green lights of creativity, a sample brainstorming session should be used. The basic ground rules of brainstorming are:

1. No critical judgment is permitted.
2. Freewheeling is welcomed (i.e., the wilder the idea, the better).
3. Quantity, not quality, is desired.
4. Combination and improvement of ideas are sought.

With these four basic rules in mind, divide the participants into groups of four to six people. Their task for 60 seconds will be to suggest all the ways they can think of to use a paper clip. Have someone in each group merely tally the *number* of ideas, not necessarily the ideas themselves. At the end of 1 minute, ask the groups to report first the number of ideas they generated, and then a sampling of some of the seemingly "crazy" or "far-out" ideas. Suggest that sometimes these "silly" ideas may well turn out to be very workable.

ALTERNATIVE METHOD

The task may be to think of ways to improve the standard (nonmechanical) lead pencil.

DISCUSSION QUESTIONS

1. What reservations do you have about the technique?
2. What kinds of problems is brainstorming best suited to?
3. What potential applications at work can you see for brainstorming?

SOURCE

Applied Imagination, Alex Osborn.

LET'S PLAY CARDS

OBJECTIVE

To form small groups in a creative way.

MATERIALS REQUIRED

Deck(s) of playing cards.

PROCEDURE

Have each person draw a card from a regular deck of playing cards. If the group is considerably smaller than 52, selectively remove as many cards as necessary to leave as many cards as there are participants. If the group exceeds 52, have additional deck(s) ready.

When you want to subdivide the group into smaller subsets, ask for each number cardholder (e.g., those with a "5") to seek each other out, and this group will form a team.

Note: Depending on the number of participants desired for each discussion period, use various ways to set them up. For example, if you want 10–12 in a group, you can ask that all Diamonds meet in one corner, Hearts in another corner, etc.

If you want two very large groups, use red and black. If you want four groups, divide them by suit. If you want to use groups of about eight, you can ask everyone with a "3" or "9" to come forward, etc. If you need a few extra people for a special activity, then designate "deuces wild" and ask them to come forward. There are countless ways to form groups with this method, and the participants enjoy something different from just "counting off by fives."

ALTERNATIVES TO "SHUT UP!"

OBJECTIVE

To quiet down a group or redirect their attention to the trainer following a period of small-group discussion.

MATERIALS REQUIRED

Items mentioned in the procedures below.

PROCEDURE

One of the most effective methods is to depersonalize the process of quieting down the group. In other words, to avoid verbal comments (e.g., "May I have your attention please," or "Will you please quiet down now?"). Instead, acquire and use some impersonal device that acts as a cue or signal to the group, and to which all have agreed. Examples of such devices include a simple whistle, an old-fashioned school bell, an oven timer, or even a small musical instrument (e.g., a recorder, triangle, harmonica, or kazoo).

Nonverbal signals can work equally well. For years the Boy Scouts of America have effectively used the simple three-fingered Boy Scout salute as an "everybody quiet" clue. The trainer only needs to catch one group's attention with a signal like this, and then the responsibility for spreading the message becomes shared by other group members.

Some trainers play a recognizable theme song on a cassette recorder.

Some trainers create three cue cards (e.g., 3–2–1, or green light–amber light–red light) that they simply display prominently to the group as a nonverbal signal to indicate the remaining time available.

Another possibility is to announce to the assembled participants at the beginning of the session that you will tell your best humorous stories in the first minute following every coffee break and small-group session. However, you will speak very softly, so that only those who are quiet can hear the stories!

SOURCE

Bob Pike, Eden Prairie, MN, and others.

Audience Energizers

TOMBSTONE PLANNING

```
┌─────────────────────┐
│      HERE LIES       │
│       • • •          │
│     GOOD OLD         │
│       FRED           │
│   A GREAT BIG ROCK   │
│   FELL ON HIS HEAD   │
│       R.I.P.         │
│    ⌐══════⌐           │
└─────────────────────┘
```

OBJECTIVES

To encourage participants to open up and disclose something meaningful about themselves.

To encourage participants to circulate among other group members during breaks.

MATERIALS REQUIRED

Tent cards and magic markers; perhaps an illustration or two drawn on overhead projector slides.

PROCEDURE

Provide everyone with tent cards (e.g., 5 × 8-inch index cards folded in half) and the opportunity to use a magic marker. Have participants print their names on the front of the tent cards (this gives them the chance to write a nickname such as "Liz" instead of the formal "Elizabeth" that may have appeared on their registration materials.)

Now instruct everyone to "Design your own inscription for your future tombstone." This should be a brief phrase, couplet, or limerick that in some way provides a commentary on their lives, their achievements, their characters, or their relationships. Examples may range from a cryptic "Ted is dead," to the emotion-dripping statement, "I told you I was sick, George!"

Now move on to your normal agenda for the session, reminding participants that they may roam around the room during refreshment breaks to inspect others' tombstone inscriptions.

DISCUSSION QUESTIONS

1. What inscriptions most caught your attention? What are they telling you?

2. If you now had the chance to design a new inscription, what would it be? (Note: In a 2- or 3-day program, you may wish to give people the chance to "wipe their slates clean" every day, and send new signals to their coparticipants.)

THE WALKING BILLBOARD

OBJECTIVE

To provide a novel way to stimulate participants to mingle and share key information with each other.

MATERIALS REQUIRED

Flip chart paper and a marker for each participant; masking tape.

PROCEDURE

Give the group two or three questions to answer about themselves. Display these on an overhead transparency or flip chart for all to see. Examples might include:

a. What is your favorite food?

b. What is your pet peeve?

c. What is the best book you've recently read?

d. What is your all-time favorite movie (or actress or actor)?

Provide every participant with a sheet of flip chart paper and a marker. Ask them to place their names at the top, and then their answers to the two or three questions posed.

Now (and this will produce some laughter) using masking tape, tell participants to help each other to attach the sheets to the writers' shoulders (they will look like walking billboards).

Then invite them all to walk around the room and discover who everyone is. (Further exploration of what was written is encouraged.)

Tell the group that they have the opportunity to design their own get-acquainted session. Ask them to propose major factors that they would like to discover about other participants in the session. List these for all to see.

Ask for a quick show of hands regarding the three most useful items from the items generated. Using a rough tabulation, select the two or three items receiving the greatest support, and identify those for the group.

Continue with the exercise by processing it as described in the procedures above.

DISCUSSION QUESTIONS

1. What are your reactions to this group-designed method of icebreaking?

2. Now that we've done this activity once, what new categories of information would you like to seek (and share!) if we were to repeat it later in the program?

TIP

You may have to put a stop to the mingling.

SOURCE

Mary DeVine, Phoenix, AZ.

"NEW DIRECTIONS" IN LEARNING

OBJECTIVES

To demonstrate to the group that prior learning (knowledge, skills, and attitudes) has a powerful and often negative effect on their capacity and willingness to adopt new learning.

To explore ways to facilitate the "unlearning" process.

MATERIALS REQUIRED

A handout or overhead transparency showing the old and the new directions (see page 129).

PROCEDURE

Present the group with a handout or visual display showing the new directions you would like to have them learn (see page 129). Give them several minutes to absorb the connection between the "old" way and the "new" way. When all are ready, have them set aside their handouts and stand up, facing the front of the room.

Test them on their "new directions" by calling out the old directions and seeing how many of them successfully point in the new directions. (*Note:* If you wish to confound them further, line them up in two rows facing each other!) Give them ten commands, and ask them to keep score of their accuracy.

What can you do to help your participants unlearn the old, thus better preparing them to learn the new?

SOURCE

John W. Newstrom, "The Management of Unlearning: Exploding the 'Clean Slate' Fallacy," *Training and Development Journal,* August 1983, pp. 36–39.

NEW DIRECTIONS IN LEARNING

Old Directions	NEW DIRECTIONS
UP	RIGHT
DOWN	REAR
LEFT	DOWN
RIGHT	FRONT
FRONT	UP
REAR	LEFT

STOP THE MUSIC!

OBJECTIVES

To energize a group after lunch.

To enable participants to relax and get acquainted.

MATERIALS REQUIRED

Question cards; music; nominal prizes.

PROCEDURE

Prepare questions (one short question on each card) about the organization or topic being presented.

Set up the meeting room in your favorite style, with extra space around each chair. (When starting the exercise, remove all extra chairs and one more.)

Describe the activity to participants. Have the participants walk around the room while you play upbeat music. After 20–30 seconds, stop the music. The participants should now all scramble for chairs. Give the lucky person left standing a card and have him or her answer the question.

Remove one chair and continue playing for four or five more turns.

TIP

The exercise may be stopped at any time. Don't spend too much time, as its main purpose is to energize the group.

COMMENT

After the exercise, give prizes (tapes, candy, handouts, etc.) to those who answered questions, with the comment that often the person who looks like a loser is the winner in the long run.

SOURCE

Ginger G. Derekson, Unlimited Futures Consulting, Owensboro, KY.

A READ AND DO TEST

OBJECTIVE

To show, in a humorous way, that people often fail to read and/or follow directions.

MATERIALS REQUIRED

Copies of the Read and Do test on page 135 and pencils or pens for all participants.

PROCEDURE

Distribute a copy of the Read and Do test to each participant. Ask them to keep the test face down until everyone has a copy. Explain that this is a timed test with a maximum time of 3 minutes allowed to complete the task. Offer no further instructions of any kind. Then state "Okay? Ready, set, go!"

A READ AND DO TEST

TIME LIMIT: 3 MINUTES
CAN YOU FOLLOW INSTRUCTIONS?

1. Read all that follows before doing anything.
2. Write your name in the upper right-hand corner of this page.
3. Circle the word "corner" in sentence two.
4. Draw five small squares in the upper left-hand corner of this page.
5. Put an "X" on each square.
6. Put a circle around each square.
7. Sign your name under line 5.
8. After your name, write "yes, yes, yes."
9. Put a circle around number 7.
10. Put an "X" in the lower left-hand corner of this page.
11. Draw a triangle around the "X" you just made.
12. Call out your first name when you get to this point in the test.
13. If you think that you have followed directions carefully to this point, call out, "I have!"
14. On the reverse side of this paper, add 6950 and 9805.
15. Put a circle around your answer.
16. Count out loud, in your normal speaking voice, from 10 to 1.
17. Put three small pin or pencil holes in the top of this page.
18. If you are the first person to get this far, yell out, "I am the first person to get to this spot and I am the leader in following directions."
19. Say out loud, "I am nearly finished. I have followed directions."
20. Now that you have finished reading carefully, do only those things called for in the sentences numbered 1 and 2. Did you read everything on this page before doing anything?

Note: *Please be quiet and watch the others follow directions.*

THE HIDDEN TRIANGLES

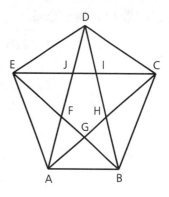

OBJECTIVE

To discourage participants from jumping to early conclusions before careful analysis of the total picture from many angles.

MATERIALS REQUIRED

Transparency and overhead projector or flip chart.

PROCEDURE

Display the figure from page 139 to the group. Direct them to count the number of triangles portrayed there. After a few minutes, ask for audience reports on how many they found in the diagram. Then proceed to explain that there are a total of 35, as follows:

KEY

1. There are 10 small single triangles (without any intersecting lines in them, e.g., AFG);
2. There are 5 tall triangles (each with an external side as a base, and containing five pieces, e.g., ABD);
3. There are 5 long-base triangles (each with three pieces, e.g., ACJ);
4. There are 5 triangles with two exterior sides (each with three pieces, e.g., EAB);
5. There are 10 triangles with two small triangles inside, e.g., ABF.

DISCUSSION QUESTIONS

1. Why didn't each of you discover all 35 triangles on your own?
2. How does the lack of a systematic approach cause us problems in our work or personal lives?

SOURCE

James Ramseyer, Dow Corning, Midland, MI.

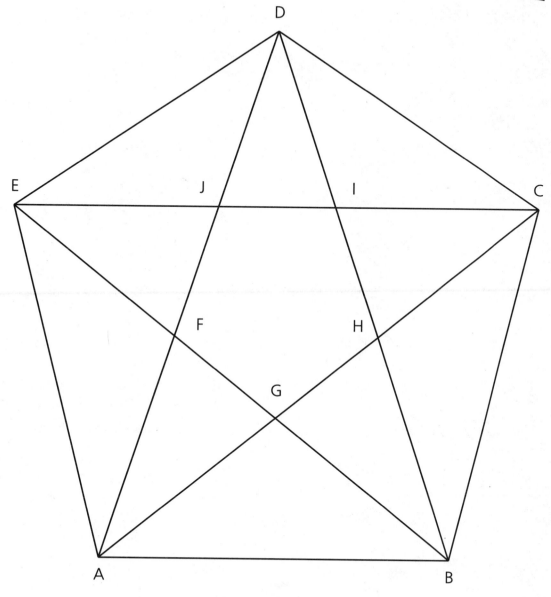

DON'T PUSH ME!

OBJECTIVE

To illustrate the importance of passive resistance.

PROCEDURE

This exercise is particularly appropriate when participants need a quick break during long sessions. It allows them to stand and move around a bit, but keeps them centered on the material. Ask participants to stand and pair off, facing their partners about three feet away. Designate one person in each pair as "A" and the other as "B." Each person places his or her hands against the hands of the partner. Hands should be at shoulder height with palms open and forward.

Tell attendees to press their hands against their partners' hands with firm and equal pressure. Ask partner "A" to remove hands quickly—and without warning—any time in the next few moments.

After all "A" partners have done so, repeat the process, but with partners "B" pulling back at their discretion.

DISCUSSION QUESTIONS

1. What was your reaction when your partner pulled away?
2. What was your feeling when you no longer felt any resistance?
3. How many of you seemed to "fall" into your partner's space when he or she stopped resisting?

4. Have you observed situations when people have actually "gained" by removing some of the "pressures" we place on others? Please describe.

5. Under what conditions should we "push," and when should we learn to "give in"?

SOURCE

Carol Klein-Zemp, Phoenix, AZ.

STAND UP AND PAT DOWN

OBJECTIVE

To create spontaneous breaks in long presentations.

PROCEDURE

1. Early in the session select one or two "Break Managers" from participants who volunteer for the job. Tell participants that Break Managers will determine when the group will take brief breaks.

2. Whenever the Break Managers believe the participants are getting a bit tired, or you are getting a bit boring, they are to stand up. This signals others to also stand up (if they'd like) and take a 30-second stretch break. Whenever the Break Managers and others stand up, you momentarily stop your presentation. This generally creates a lot of humor and goodwill with the group and sometimes gives them a chance to tell you (in a good-natured way) they think you're on a tangent.

3. In a long presentation, during the second or third stand-up break, encourage people to "pat down," that is to massage the backs of their own necks, legs, arms, etc. and to stretch or loosen up physically. This helps people feel more awake and energized.

4. In a very long presentation, during the third or fourth stand-up break, encourage people to "pat down" or massage one another's shoulders and backs. This is usually both fun and refreshing for most participants, although those who are more inhibited may choose to take the break without participating in the massage.

SOURCE

Adapted by Dr. Ed Kur from games played by Joel Weldon and Jeanie Cochran.

LEADER OF THE BAND

OBJECTIVE

To provide an opportunity for participants to loosen up after a period of intense activity or discussion or passive absorption of a lecture or video.

MATERIALS REQUIRED

Tape player and music tapes.

PROCEDURE:

Pick a time when the group's energy seems particularly low.

Call for a unique (non-coffee, non-use of restroom) break. Ask all participants to stand up and make sufficient room around themselves so as not to interfere with free movement of their arms.

Tell them that they have won the right to be "The Leader of the Band" and direct the world-famous Philadelphia Orchestra for the next 5 minutes. You might also wish to tell them that mock-direction of an orchestra is believed to be excellent emotional release and physical (cardiovascular) exercise. Then play a selection and ask them all to simultaneously lead the orchestra.

Note: This works best if you have carefully selected the music. We recommend that the music be familiar to all, so they will know what is coming next. The music should be relatively fast-paced to stimulate energetic directing (Sousa marches or even Strauss waltzes work well); also, music with a variety of speeds and volumes tends to elicit different directing styles.

DISCUSSION QUESTIONS

1. How do you feel now that you have directed the orchestra?

2. How many of you are likely to go home and direct music from your own record collection?

3. What is there about the activity of orchestra directing that gives us permission to wave our arms and move our bodies in a refreshing way—something we might otherwise not be inclined to do?

APPROXIMATE TIME REQUIRED

5 minutes.

SOURCE

Art Richardson, Le Mars, IA.

HOW MANY TREES ARE IN AN APPLE?

OBJECTIVE

To demonstrate that often it is useful to immerse yourself in a problem so that you can see all of its dimensions.

MATERIALS REQUIRED

Picture of an apple tree; one apple per person; napkins; paring knives.

PROCEDURE

Display a picture of an apple tree to the group. Suggest that it is a relatively easy task for anyone to determine the number of apples on a tree (through observation and careful counting). Consequently, the task lends itself to completion on an individual basis.

Some tasks, however, require immersion into them before the answer can be obtained. Distribute an apple to each participant. Ask them to determine how many trees are (potentially) within each apple. The solution, of course, lies in dissecting each apple (they may eat them, if they wish) and counting the number of seeds found.

DISCUSSION QUESTIONS

1. What kinds of problems have you encountered that are of a similar nature?
2. What techniques have you found useful to aid you in the process of immersion?

APPROXIMATE TIME REQUIRED

5–10 minutes.

SOURCE

Avery Willis, Baptist Sunday School Board, Nashville, TN.

8

Encouraging Audience Participation

THE DOLLAR EXCHANGE

OBJECTIVE

To encourage a climate for open exchange of ideas among participants.

MATERIALS REQUIRED

None for the first procedure. Play money for the alternative.

PROCEDURE

Ask for the loan of a dollar from a member of the group. Displaying it prominently in one hand, proceed to ask for the loan of a second dollar from another participant. Then carefully repay the first loaner with the second dollar and repay the second loaner with the first dollar. Then ask the rhetorical question, "Is either of these persons now richer than before?" (Neither, of course, is.) Then point out to the group that by contrast had two ideas been shared as readily, not only the respective givers, but *all* participants, would be richer in experience than they were previously.

ALTERNATIVE

Give each participant one (or more) pieces of preprinted play money. Let them exchange the money first to experience the lack of enrichment that ensues. Then let each person write an idea on the play money and either circulate the bills or post them in a conspicuous place where members may inspect them at their leisure (during coffee breaks).

DISCUSSION QUESTIONS

1. What factors *prevent* us from sharing useful ideas and insights with others?
2. What forces *encourage* us to share ideas with others in meetings, seminars, and presentations?

IDEA EXCHANGE

OBJECTIVE

To encourage participation and sharing of ideas.

MATERIALS REQUIRED

Cards, tickets, or play money.

PROCEDURE

Each participant is given play money bills (or 3 × 5-inch cards) that are either mailed out in advance or distributed the day before the first session. They are told to write a single idea on each bill, for a total of five of the best ideas (preferably organized around a single issue or problem, such as, "How to encourage recycling or carpooling," or suggestions for a sales campaign theme or slogan). Names are signed, and they are told that the ideas will be competitively judged and shared.

At the first session, the bills or cards are collected and shuffled in a box. Each attendee draws five bills or cards (not their own) and selects the one believed to be the best, signs his or her name below that of the idea's originator, and forwards it to the presenter.

Outside of the session, the presenter identifies all of the double nominees and records them on a handout, overhead transparency, or flip chart paper.

At an appropriate time in the program, all of these double nominees are then read aloud and audience reaction may be assessed by a show of hands on a five- or ten-point scale (judged anonymously). After all the ideas have been assessed, the top three (or five) qualify for prizes, which are awarded to both the originator and the nominator. The rest of the group also "wins" by virtue of being exposed to a large number of successful ideas.

IF YOU HAVE MORE TIME

Instead of tabulating the nominations outside of the presentation, read all the nominations aloud during the presentation, conduct the audience vote, and award prizes.

DISCUSSION QUESTIONS

1. What useful *content* has been gained? (Dependent on the problem or issue posed.)

2. What useful *process* transpired? (Widespread participation, a spirit of cooperation and cohesion, etc.)

3. How would the same technique be used on the job? (Ask employees for safety ideas, work simplification suggestions, job enrichment approaches, etc.)

SWAP SHOP

OBJECTIVES

To cultivate a number of new ideas.

To encourage group participation.

MATERIALS REQUIRED

Three sets of flash cards (5 × 8-inch index cards), each set numbered from one to ten.

PROCEDURE

Everyone is told *in advance* to bring at least one idea, exercise, activity, etc., to the next session. These should be focused around some central theme (e.g., how to improve quality, cut costs, reward outstanding performance, etc.).

As each person describes his or her idea to the group, a panel of "experts" (three selected participants) instantly "rates" the idea by holding up a prepared flash card (1 to 10, with 10 being high). The presenter tabulates each total and announces the winners at the end of the time period.

DISCUSSION QUESTIONS

1. How many people gained at least one useful new idea today?
2. Did this process spark any additional ideas in your mind?
3. Can you think of some other areas in which this method can be applied?
4. What are some other variations on this technique?

STAY ON THE BALL

OBJECTIVES

To stimulate participants to be attentive and focus on active listening during a discussion.

To demonstrate that active involvement in the session by each participant is desired by the presenter and can also be enjoyable.

MATERIALS REQUIRED

A soft sponge ball.

PROCEDURE

1. Take out a soft, catchable ball (e.g., a soft sponge ball). Select a participant and throw it back and forth to that one person for a minute or two.

2. After the pattern has been firmly established, invite the other participants to join. Make sure that the ball passes back and forth among the participants and only occasionally to yourself. Observe carefully to make sure that no one is neglected and direct the ball to them if it happens. Continue this for a few minutes until a clear pattern of cross-group interaction is established.

3. Engage the group in brief discussion, revolving around the following questions.

DISCUSSION QUESTIONS

1. How did you feel when only one person and I were playing catch?

2. Did you observe more spontaneity, smiles, and overall involvement when the entire group was participating? Why?

3. Is there an important analogy here—that we can learn from each other (not just the presenter), but only if we all agree to become actively involved in both the listening and contributing processes?

SOURCE

M. Kane, Imperial Life Assurance Co., Toronto, Ontario, Canada.

THE COMPANY STORE CATALOG

OBJECTIVE

To encourage active oral participation (depth and breadth).

MATERIALS REQUIRED

Play money, chips, or some other suitable form of currency; an array of catalog items.

PROCEDURE

Obtain or create some form of distributable currency, such as play money from a Monopoly game or a set of poker chips (be sure to establish the relative values of red, white, blue, and yellow chips in advance).

Create a "Company Store Catalog" by accumulating a number of potentially valued prizes for the session participants. These might include gift certificates from the company cafeteria worth any amount from a free cup of coffee to free lunch; a coffee mug with the company logo; a free book relevant to the topic (e.g., *What Every Superior Should Know,* by Lester Bittel and John Newstrom, or *Supervisory Communication* by Edward E. Scannell); or more imaginative items such as lunch with the CEO in the executive cafeteria, or two free theater tickets, or a free round of golf. Be imaginative!

Inform the audience of your participative expectations, and the array of rewards available. Then begin rewarding the appropriate behaviors by promptly distributing dollars or chips when the participants' actions warrant it.

Later, when basic patterns are established, you can further shape desired behaviors by increasing the size of the reward offered or making a group reward (e.g., dollars for everyone) contingent upon a specific behavior (e.g., analytical vs. regurgitative responses).

At the end of the session, allow participants a few minutes to browse through your "Company Store Catalog" and "buy" the items of their choice.

Allow 5 minutes to explain the process, and 10–15 minutes at the end to sell items.

DISCUSSION QUESTIONS

1. To what degree did the offer of "rewards" affect your willingness to participate?
2. Did the reward system distract you in any way? To what degree did it contribute to your learning or retention?

SOURCE

John Newstrom, Duluth, MN.

EXPECTATIONS FULFILLED!

OBJECTIVE

To glean from participants at the start of a presentation the particular expectations they may have for the program.

MATERIALS REQUIRED

Blank sheets of paper and pencils for all participants.

PROCEDURE

At the beginning of any new topic within a presentation, give a blank sheet of paper to each person. Instruct them to write on the page any and all matters or questions that they have about the subject to be discussed. These may be in the form of questions, issues, or concerns they expect to have on the respective segment.

After a few minutes, collect all the unsigned sheets. Glance through them quickly and summarize some of the more relevant issues or themes, suggesting that these will be addressed. If a few questions are totally outside the scope of that particular phase, thank participants for the question and advise them of the situation. Time permitting, if the area in question is one in which other participants may have expertise or interest, suggest they get together during break times.

Set the papers aside until near the end of that segment. At that time, arbitrarily hand out the sheets to participants in random fashion. Ask them to read the questions on their sheets, and then attempt to respond to the questions. If the question posed is particularly difficult, ask others in the group for assistance.

Allow 5 minutes at the start of the program, 15 minutes at the close.

DISCUSSION QUESTIONS

1. Did you get your most critical question(s) answered?
2. Did you increase your own ability to answer someone else's questions?

SOURCE

Donald W. H. McDonald, Auckland, New Zealand.

THE COAT

OBJECTIVES

To demonstrate the danger of making assumptions about a participant's background knowledge and common vocabulary.

To illustrate the advantage of modeling, demonstration, and interaction over one-way communication.

MATERIALS REQUIRED

A jacket, match box, or other alternative prop.

PROCEDURE

Lay a jacket on the table. Select a "volunteer" and inform him or her that you don't know what the jacket is or what to do with it. The volunteer's task is to train you in the jacket's use as quickly as possible. The "trainer" will often engage in telling behaviors whose effectiveness can be distorted by slow learner behaviors on the part of the "trainee" (e.g., grabbing the pocket when told to grab the collar, or inserting the arm up the sleeve in a reverse direction). The difficulty of completing the assignment can be further exaggerated by depriving the trainer of visual feedback, having the trainer turn his or her back to the trainee. After a brief time period of minimal progress, the class can be asked for its assistance. A fruitful alternative, of course, is to *show* the trainee how to use the jacket. This can effectively illustrate the merits of the classic Job Instruction Training (J.I.T.) approach, which is to:

1. Explain how to do it.
2. Demonstrate how to do it.

3. Request an explanation of how to do it.

4. Invite the trainee to do it.

ALTERNATIVES

The same process can be used with other articles of clothing (e.g., shoes) or even with a box of wooden matches (with the goal of lighting one).

DISCUSSION QUESTIONS

1. Why did the trainer initially have a difficult time with the task of training? (Because of assumptions about prior knowledge and common vocabulary, because of limited patience with a slow learner doing a "simple" task, or because of one-way communication.)

2. What are the benefits of demonstration? (Add the sense of sight, and the words take on additional meaning.)

3. What are the benefits of feedback? (Can gauge progress, understanding, and satisfaction of trainees.)

SOURCE

R. K. Gaumnitz, University of Minnesota (Minneapolis).

GRAFFITI FEEDBACK BOARDS

OBJECTIVE

To provide an anonymous outlet for ongoing participant reactions.

MATERIALS REQUIRED

Flip chart or similar medium on which to write; markers or chalk.

PROCEDURE

Most reaction-based evaluation systems gather data at the end of a session or program, or possibly at a future date. The motivation to treat these seriously is lessened by the fact that changes will occur too late to improve the quality of the current session.

An informal alternative is the use of graffiti boards. Through the use of poster boards, flip charts, or chalkboards, participants may express (ventilate) a variety of observations, reactions, ideas, or emotions to the presenter or the group. This may be done on a relatively anonymous basis. Topics may be provided at the top (e.g., "presentation content," "physical facilities," etc.) or the feedback may be solicited on a totally unstructured basis. In any case, an important outlet for emotional and intellectual catharsis has been provided.

DISCUSSION QUESTIONS

1. How many of you agree with the comment made about _____?

2. What is the basis for the various comments?

3. What corrective steps can we take *now* to change the situation?

SOURCE

Emily Hitchins, "Graffiti Provides Useful Feedback," *Training,* August, 1979, p. 12.

FEEDBACK CARDS

OBJECTIVE

To provide an expeditious method for obtaining comprehensive feedback from a group of participants.

MATERIALS REQUIRED

Cards for each participant.

PROCEDURE

Obtain poster boards with one color on one side and a second color on the other (preferably red and green). Cut them into small squares (approximately four inches per side). Distribute one to each participant.

Inform the group that the cards will be used to provide the presenter with feedback in response to his or her questions. Questions with true/false or yes/no responses work best, with green indicating true or yes, and red reflecting false or no. The entire group should then hold up their cards in response to presenter questions. Not only does this give the presenter immediate feedback on the retention and understanding in the group, but the participants can also be encouraged to look around and determine the degree of agreement with their response.

Note: This is also an effective procedure for controlling tangential discussions by participants (or even the presenter!), wherein the group members may indicate their willingness to pursue or truncate the discussion by display of the green (continue) or red (terminate) cards.

SOURCE

Dr. Richard Beatty, University of Colorado, and John Price, Prudential House, York, England.

COMPETING FOR DOLLARS

OBJECTIVE

To utilize competition and economic rewards to stimulate high audience involvement in the learning process.

MATERIALS REQUIRED

Advance list of content facts and display boards (hook and loop, magnetic, chalk, etc.); silver dollars and five-dollar bills.

PROCEDURE

Select a set of items that a participant group is to have learned (e.g., the characteristics of a new product or the components of a machine). List these along with some erroneous items on two large display boards, screens, or worksheets that are placed so the audience cannot see them.

Select two teams of two persons each to work at the boards. Their objective is to place an "X" next to each of the *correct* features.

After a brief period of time, the presenter stops the action.

The boards are then turned toward the audience, who are asked to spot errors on the boards. Members identifying a true error are awarded a silver dollar for each one spotted. Then the winning team members (those with the least errors) are awarded five dollars.

The exercise provides a spirit of competition as well as an achievement opportunity for the participants. It is, in effect, a fun way to "test" an entire group, and the camaraderie that develops often is exemplified by the "winners" buying refreshments for the "losers."

IF YOU HAVE MORE TIME

Multiple products (and lists) allow repetition of the exercise several times.

SOURCE

Jack Shepman, "Dollars for Errors," *Training,* April, 1978, pp. 11, 54.

9

Reinforcing and Reviewing Key Ideas

THE ALPHABET REVIEW

OBJECTIVE

To encourage participants to stretch their minds and their collective memories, while demonsrating that a large number of useful items were learned.

MATERIALS REQUIRED

One copy of the worksheet on page 175 for each participant.

PROCEDURE

At the beginning of the session, distribute one copy of the "Alphabet Review" worksheet to each person. Ask each participant to generate at least one significant item (a principle, concept, or conclusion) from the workshop that starts with each letter of the alphabet. Tell participants to record items as they are introduced to them. This also has the merit of cueing participants to watch for at least 26 key items throughout the session.

Note: Be flexible in allowing various adaptations of correctly-spelled words, or "borrowed" adjectives to describe a concept (such as "xcellent customer service").

Summarize the session by asking for an item that begins with A, then B, then C, etc. Participants will be surprised at the variety of items they identified for different letters.

IF YOU HAVE MORE TIME

At the end of the session, form small groups of three to five persons. Distribute one copy of the "Alphabet Review" form on page 175 to each person. Ask the teams to generate at least one significant item (a principle, concept, or conclusion) from the workshop that starts with each letter of the alphabet. Summarize the session by going from group to group asking for an item that begins with A, then B, then C, etc.

DISCUSSION QUESTIONS

1. How much difficulty did you have completing the entire list?
2. How many of you were surprised that 26 or more important items could be generated so quickly?
3. How helpful was it to work in small groups? Does this suggest the value of staying in touch with workshop participants at a later date?

SOURCE

Adapted from "Body Search" by Creative Training Techniques.

ALPHABET REVIEW

A   B

C   D

E   F

G   H

I   J

K   L

M   N

O   P

Q   R

S   T

U   V

W   X

Y   Z

THE WHEEL OF FORTUNE

OBJECTIVE

To turn a dry review exercise into a game that stimulates closer participant attention and active involvement.

MATERIALS REQUIRED

One relevant phrase, a blank transparency or flip chart with the correct number of blank spaces filled in, and a "prize" for the winner.

PROCEDURE

Select a short phrase that is appropriately related to either the meeting, the participants, or the organization. Examples could be "Six-sigma quality" or "Quality is job one" or "Teachers make the grade."

Create a blank master on handouts, flip chart, or transparency that shows the appropriate number and spacing of missing letters.

Inform the group that during the review period they will have an opportunity to play "Wheel of Fortune" (without the usual cohosts seen on TV). Then begin asking a series of answerable review questions, proceeding around the audience in systematic fashion with each successive one.

Whenever anyone answers a question correctly, they may guess a letter. If the letter belongs one or more times in the phrase, fill it in and allow that person to try to guess the phrase.

When the correct guess is finally given, award a prize to the winner and invite the class to celebrate his or her success with applause.

An example is shown on pages 179 and 181.

DISCUSSION QUESTION

How did knowing you would be playing a review game help or hinder your retention of key material?

SOURCE

Inspired by Bob Pike, Creative Training Techniques.

CLUE: "PATHS TO SURVIVAL"

Answer:

— — — — — — —, — — — — —,

— — — — — — —, — — —

— — — — —   — — —   — — —

— — — — — —   — —

— — — — — —   — — — — — —.

CLUE: "PATHS TO SURVIVAL"

Answer:

QUALITY, SPEED,

SERVICE, AND VALUE

ARE THE ROUTES TO

FUTURE SUCCESS

QUICKIE REVIEW

OBJECTIVE

To provide intermediate review checkpoints on how well participants are retaining and learning the material.

PROCEDURE

For full-day or longer programs, this technique is used to measure participant learning in an enjoyable way.

Just prior to the first scheduled break, suggest to the group that a lot of material has already been covered. To check on what they've learned so far, you're going to do a quick review. Before you break the session for coffee, etc., you need to hear *ten things they've learned so far.* Then, as rapidly as possible, asking for responses. After each one, say "Thank you, that's one" etc., until ten key points are stated.

At the end of the morning session, and just before lunch, repeat the exercise by reminding the group of the content covered and asking for seven things they've learned since the mid-morning break. Repeat the procedure at mid-afternoon break and again at final closure time.

Note: The number of things learned (to be solicited from the group) is arbitrarily chosen each time by the presenter.

DISCUSSION QUESTIONS

1. How many were surprised by the number of items the group was able to generate?
2. What is the value in learning what others considered to be the most important items?
3. In what ways was your list different from that of others?

TOP TEN REVIEW

TOP TEN LIST (MOST IMPORTANT ACTION PRINCIPLES)
1.
2.
3.
4.
5.
6.
7.
8.
9.
10.

OBJECTIVE

To encourage participants to stretch their minds and their collective memories, while demonstrating that a large number of useful items were learned during the program.

MATERIALS REQUIRED

Note cards and one worksheet for each participant.

PROCEDURE

Distribute a generous supply of small note cards to each participant at the beginning of the presentation. Ask participants to succinctly state one key action principle from the presentation on each card, as they think of them.

Collect the cards at the end of the session and promise to tabulate the results and mail the information to participants within 72 hours.

Type up the list of "Top Ten" in order of priority, and mail to the participants. This is an excellent way to reinforce the key points—*as seen through their eyes.*

IF YOU HAVE MORE TIME

Alternative A

Collect the participants' note cards prior to the final session, and have an aide quickly type them up verbatim on a single master sheet, numbering them 1, 2, 3, 4, etc. Distribute copies to each participant. Then ask them to identify a fixed number of the most meaningful ones (e.g., allow them each to identify, with a check, 10 out of a list of 37). Conduct a quick poll of the group (show of hands) for how many chose each one. Count the votes, and inform them of the results for the "Top Ten." Allow 20–30 minutes.

Alternative B

Form small groups of three to five persons, and ask each group to arrive at a consensus of the most important action principles. Give each group a copy of the Top Ten List on page 187 to record its consensus items. Allow 20–30 minutes.

DISCUSSION QUESTIONS

1. How many items did you generate?
2. How many of your items are on the master list?
3. How helpful was it to work in small groups? What insights did you gain by hearing others' opinions?

TOP TEN LIST (MOST IMPORTANT ACTION PRINCIPLES)

1.

2.

3.

4.

5.

6.

7.

8.

9.

10.

JEOPARDY

OBJECTIVE

To provide a competitive environment for the reinforcement of material presented in this or previous sessions.

MATERIALS REQUIRED

Previously prepared list of test questions; prize.

PROCEDURE

1. Separate participants into two groups.

2. Develop sets of questions, organized in categories according to the material that has previously been presented.

3. Allow one team to select a category, and ask them a question. If they are successful, award a point (or play money may be used). If they are incorrect, the other team gets a chance to answer, and may thus earn points. If neither team answers it correctly, they must look it up in the program reference material.

4. The first group to accumulate a specified number of points is declared the winner (and some recognition or prize should be awarded).

5. The major benefits provided by this format are:

   a. repetition of key material;

   b. reinforcement of effective learning;

   c. feedback to the presenter regarding the points learned well, and those on which there was difficulty on recall.

SOURCE

Dolores E. Verdi, AT&T, New Brunswick, NJ.

PASSWORD REVIEW

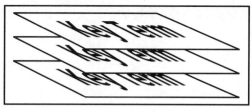

OBJECTIVES

To assess the degree of retention of key concepts among participants.

To reinforce major terms at the end of a presentation.

MATERIALS REQUIRED

Two identical decks of cards with key vocabulary terms associated with the program.

PROCEDURE

Develop a master set of key vocabulary terms associated with the program. Print each term on a separate card, and create a duplicate deck. Number the cards sequentially to assure that they remain in order.

Divide the group into two teams. Select the first two players, one from each team. They should each draw the top card from one of the decks, but not show them to their teammates.

One player starts first, by giving a verbal clue (e.g., a rhyming word, a synonym, a single-word clue) to the teammates. The teammates, in collaboration, may make one guess within a short, fixed time period. If they are correct, they get ten points. If they are incorrect, the second team's player may offer a new clue, and that team's players get a chance to guess for nine possible points. Play continues on the word until ten guesses are made, or the term has been guessed.

Points are recorded for the team with the correct guess, and play continues to the next set of players and words in the deck. The team with the greatest number of points at the end of a given time period (or the end of the deck) wins, and should be given a prize of some nature.

DISCUSSION QUESTIONS

1. Which terms gave the group the greatest difficulty? Why?

2. Which terms would you now like to have clarified?

TIP

The time required for this exercise is dependent on the number of terms, familiarity of the players with the terms, time limit placed on each guessing round, and the players' clue-giving capacity.

POSITIVE REINFORCEMENT FOR PARTICIPANTS

OBJECTIVE

To demonstrate that positive reinforcement increases the probability that a given behavior will appear again.

MATERIALS REQUIRED

Advance selection of reinforcers (e.g., cans, slogans printed on Frisbees, baseball caps, T-shirts, bumper stickers, drink tickets, dollar bills).

PROCEDURE

Reinforcement theory predicts that if a given behavior is followed by a positive consequence, that behavior will increase in its subsequent frequency. The person in control must make sure the consequences are contingent upon performance, and that the consequences are positive for the recipient.

Joel Weldon has perfected the process in his motivational presentations, and other presenters can borrow directly from his technique. Joel has produced stick-on labels for small cans that say, "Success comes in cans, not in cannots." When hearing the catchy little phrase and viewing the take-home reward that can be theirs for displaying the appropriate behavior, the participants enjoy the exercise and respond accordingly. Whenever a person contributes an insightful comment or breaks up the room with a humorous remark, Joel reinforces that person with a "can," and the remainder of the group tries that much harder to obtain their "cans."

In general, the key is to:

1. Identify something that will be generally desired (e.g., free drink tickets for the cocktail party).
2. Let the group know that these rewards are available (either through prior announcement or after the first appropriate behavior).
3. Give the rewards out liberally, but conditionally.

DISCUSSION QUESTIONS

At the end of the session, a brief presentation can be made on positive reinforcement by focusing the discussion around the following questions:

1. Why did people participate so actively?
2. What would have happened if the presenter had withheld a reward one time?
3. What if the presenter had chosen the wrong reinforcement for the group?
4. What other applications of positive reinforcement can the group see?

SOURCE

Joel H. Weldon, Scottsdale, AZ.

EVEN PRESENTERS ERR SOMETIMES

OBJECTIVES

To stimulate participants to focus carefully on what the presenter is doing and saying.

To motivate participants to reflect on ways that they could improve on what is being taught.

MATERIALS REQUIRED

None, except for any props (bad visuals, etc.).

PROCEDURE

The following discussion assumes that you are delivering a session on "effective presentations," but could be equally adaptable to many other topics, wherever demonstration is appropriate. It is especially useful in those (frequent!) contexts where some participants feel that they already know most of the answers (and probably do have some expertise).

Begin the session by exhibiting several of the most common mistakes that presenters might make. For example, you might:

1. Be late.
2. Be unorganized.
3. Maintain poor eye contact.
4. Speak in a monotone.
5. Forget to plug in the projector.
6. Not bring enough handouts.
7. Have poor visual aids.
8. Etc.

After several minutes of this, stop and have the group identify all the things that you did wrong. These can be listed on a flip chart, followed by discussion of the correct ways for presenters to act. The visual impact of seeing the errors in action is powerful, and it is a useful way to stimulate discussion within the group.

SOURCE

Ron Babitz, Meijer, Inc., Grand Rapids, MI.

10

Winding Down: Memorable Closing Activities

COLLECTING POSITIVE STROKES

A tip for your success:

I wish you would ...

OBJECTIVE

To end a presentation or program on a positive note.

MATERIALS REQUIRED

One large envelope and one set of cards per participant.

PROCEDURE

1. Provide each group member with a roster of names and one blank 3 × 5-inch card for each participant. At the beginning of the session, instruct them to observe their colleagues' behavior closely, and write one positive remark about each participant on a card. (The presenter may also choose to be a participant in this process—both as a contributor and as a participant.)

2. Toward the end of the program, collect the cards (be sure the intended recipients' names are on them), sort them into the appropriate envelopes and distribute them to each person. Allow adequate time to let each person scan quickly through their cards. This allows all participants to leave the session with some positive feelings about themselves, even though the program may have been stressful.

ALTERNATIVE

1. Ask participants to provide each other participant with "One tip for your success."

2. Ask them to complete this sentence for each participant: "I wish you would…"

DISCUSSION QUESTIONS

1. If time permits, ask each participant to read aloud the single card that made him or her feel the best.

2. Ask each participant to read aloud the single card that most surprised (or confused) him or her.

TIP

This activity is best suited for groups of 12 or fewer. If you use the activity with larger groups, allow more time to distribute the envelopes to each participant, as well as for participants to read the cards they have received.

SOURCE

Lee A. Beckner, Cameron Iron Works, Inc., Houston, TX.

POSITIVE STROKES

OBJECTIVE

To have the participants leave a session with positive affirmations. Primarily designed for workshop sessions (25 or fewer participants).

MATERIALS REQUIRED

3 × 5-inch index cards.

PROCEDURE

Two or three times during the session, ask each person to fill out a 3 × 5-inch card about each other participant, completing sentences such as "The thing I like best about (name) is ..." or, "The biggest improvement I saw in (name) was... ."

At the end of the day, the (folded) cards are passed out. Each participant then leaves the session with a number of positive affirmations.

IF YOU HAVE MORE TIME

Read the cards aloud and then give them to the named person.

SOURCE

Bob Bloch, Lenox, MA.

TIME TO SHARE

OBJECTIVES

To let individuals give positive strokes to others.

To subtly get participants to recognize positive qualities of others.

PROCEDURE

After instructing the group to pair off, introduce the session by suggesting we all need and crave recognition and positive strokes.

Have each person tell his or her partner **one** of the following:

1. one physical feature that is particularly nice;

2. one or two personality traits that are unusually pleasant;

3. one or two talents or skills that are noteworthy.

Suggest that each person record his or her partner's feelings, thoughts, and feedback and save them to read on a "bummer day."

IF YOU HAVE MORE TIME

Have each person give the partner a compliment on two or all three of the topic areas in the Procedures section.

DISCUSSION QUESTIONS

1. Why is it difficult for many of us to give another person a compliment?

2. Why is it that some people are quick to give a negative comment, but seldom, if ever, have anything nice to say about people?

3. "People tend to behave as we tend to think they should behave." Do you agree or disagree? Why?

TIP

This activity is best used when participants have previously had the opportunity to share and interact with each other.

SOURCE

Dr. Robert Lindberg, University of Texas at San Antonio.

VALUE ADDED

OBJECTIVE

To identify the areas of job responsibilities that do and do not add value to the organization.

MATERIALS REQUIRED

Paper and pencils or pens for all participants.

PROCEDURE

Pose the following questions to the group: Suppose that you had more time to do the activities that you honestly believe you are better trained, more experienced, etc., to do—activities that you believe would definitely mean "Value Added" to your organization, but that right now, you just can't do. *What are those activities?*

Ask participants to think seriously about the question and write down one such value-added activity on a piece of paper. Allow 1 minute for this, and then ask the second key question:

Some activities you perform probably don't utilize your talents as much as they could. These activities are not considered Value Added, but they seem to consume a large portion of your time and energy. These are the kinds of job activities that you have to do, but frankly, you wish you did not have to do so often, or even at all. *What are those activities?* Again, ask the group to ponder the question, and write out one such activity. (Allow 1 minute.)

Subdivide the total group into pairs and ask them to share their individual comments and insights into Value Added activities for the next 2 minutes.

IF YOU HAVE MORE TIME

Give participants 5 minutes to think seriously about the question and list several value-added activities on a piece of paper.

Then give participants 5 minutes to think about and list several non-value-added activities that they currently perform.

Subdivide the total group into triads and ask them to share their individual comments and insights into Value Added activities for the next 5-10 minutes.

DISCUSSION QUESTIONS

1. What are some of the tasks you feel you could be doing to help your organization improve?
2. What can you *do* about the items in question 1?
3. What are some activities you could *forget* about?
4. Are there some activities that you could or perhaps should delegate to others?

SOURCE

Frank Helton, Fountain Hills, AZ.

TEST YOUR CONSTRAINTS

OBJECTIVE

To stimulate participants to identify, classify, and mentally test which factors are most significant in keeping them from starting or stopping something.

MATERIALS REQUIRED

Paper and pencils or pens for all participants.

PROCEDURE

1. Explain that people are often boxed in by various constraints. However, it is our perception of these limitations that creates the most significant barriers, and these perceptions need to be explored.

2. Give participants 1 minute to think of something that they would like to either start doing or stop doing.

3. Give participants 1 minute to list things that now prevent them from accomplishing their objective. Then give them 2 minutes to categorize the obstacles they listed as:

    a. realistic and rigid (e.g., upper-management edicts);

    b. moderately firm (e.g., standard policies and practices that are usually inviolable);

    c. flexible (implicit procedures or interpersonal/intergroup relations);

    d. illusionary (partly based on facts but largely embellished by our imagination).

4. Point out that one organization (General Electric) discovered that over 95 percent of the constraints identified by its foremen and first-line supervisors were classified as either flexible or illusionary.

5. Encourage them to test their limits, to be willing to experiment, take a risk, and see what happens.

DISCUSSION QUESTIONS

1. What kinds of things did you identify that you would like to start or stop doing?
2. What were some of the illusionary constraints that you identified?
3. Give an example of an action plan for overcoming one of the constraints.

SOURCE

Richard D. Colvin, General Electric Management Development Institute, as described in "Increasing Personal Effectiveness," *Training and Development Journal,* January 1978, pp. 30–33.

I'M GONNA WRITE MYSELF A LETTER...

OBJECTIVE

To provide a formal method of follow-up and self-contracting for behavior change following a skills-oriented or personal or professional growth presentation.

MATERIALS REQUIRED

Handouts, envelopes, and stamps for all participants.

PROCEDURE

Toward the end of your presentation, distribute copies of the form on page 211 to each participant.

Tell the group that you realize that a lot of material has been covered and now it's up to them to apply the learning to their jobs.

Give them sufficient time to fill out the forms, and then distribute blank envelopes which the participants will address to themselves. Have the participants insert the forms in their own envelopes, seal them, and pass them back to you.

Place postage on the envelopes and mail them to the participants about two to three weeks after the program.

DISCUSSION QUESTIONS

1. What impact will writing these contracts have on you and your behavior?
2. How many think that you will be successful in doing the things you told yourself you'd do?
3. What kinds of barriers will make it difficult or even impossible for you to carry out your promise?

SOURCE

Lou Hampton, Washington, D.C.; and Mary Broad and John Newstrom, *Transfer of Training* (Reading, MA: Addison-Wesley, 1992).

MEMORANDUM

HANDOUT

TO: _____

FROM: _____

SUBJECT: CONTRACT WITH MYSELF

DATE: _____

The most important or significant ideas that I've learned/thought/heard/ while at this presentation are

_____

_____

As a result of these ideas, I intend to do the following things within the next 30 days:

_____

_____

_____

By doing these things, I will achieve the following results:

_____

_____

Note: Change these questions to more accurately fit the content of the respective presentation as necessary.

IF YOU WANT MY OPINION ...

OBJECTIVE

To encourage honest, anonymous feedback from participants for trainer evaluation at the conclusion of a presentation.

MATERIALS REQUIRED

Two flip charts and several colored markers.

PROCEDURE

Place two flip charts at the rear of the meeting room.

On the first flip chart, write these words:

"Here are some things we especially valued about this program..."

On the second flip chart, write these words:

"Here are some suggestions as to how this program could be even better..."

Tell participants that you will be leaving the room for the next 5 minutes and you sincerely ask their honest evaluation of the program. Ask them to write down their individual responses to the two questions posed. Explain that they should not sign their names, but you would appreciate their specific suggestions and assessment.

Leave the room for at least 5 minutes. If participants are still writing their comments after 5 minutes, allow a few more minutes. When you return, thank the group for their suggestions and comments.

Tear off the flip charts and return to your office. You may choose to type up the comments and distribute them to relevant audiences (e.g., your boss or the program participants), or you may simply study them yourself to identify any relevant themes or constructive comments affecting things within your control. Then, celebrate your success, and change something that needs improvement!

SOURCE

Christopher P. Davies, Jozsefhegyi, Hungary.

about the authors

An active member of the National Speakers Association, **Edward E. Scannell** has given more than one thousand presentations, seminars, and workshops across the United States and in several overseas venues.

Equally involved in both civic and professional organizations, he has served on the boards of directors of a number of groups, including the Tempe Chamber of Commerce, the American Society for Training and Development (ASTD), Meeting Professionals International (MPI), and the National Speakers Association. He was elected National President of ASTD in 1982 and later served a two-year term as the Executive Chairman of the International Federation of Training and Development Organizations.

He has written or co-authored several books and over one hundred articles in the fields of human resource management, communication, creativity, meeting planning, management, and teambuilding. His best-selling *Games Trainers Play* series (McGraw-Hill), co-authored with John W. Newstrom, is used by speakers, trainers, and meeting planners around the world.

Formerly the Director of the University Conference Bureau at Arizona State University, Mr. Scannell also taught at the ASU College of Business and at the University of Northern Iowa. He is currently serving as the Director of the Center for Professional Development and Training in Scottsdale, Arizona.

Dr. John W. Newstrom is a university professor, noted author, and consultant to organizations in the areas of training and supervisory development. He is currently a professor of human resource management in the School of Business and Economics at the University of Minnesota, Duluth, where he teaches courses and workshops in the fields of organizational change, human resource development, management, and interpersonal and group relations. He has conducted training programs on a wide range of topics for organizations including 3M Co., Lakehead Pipeline, LTV Steel Mining, Blandin Paper Co., Diamond Tool, Minnesota Power, Clyde Iron, City of Scottsdale, Armour-Dial, and St. Luke's Hospital.

John has been active in the American Society for Training and Development (ASTD) since 1971 and has been a popular speaker, appearing before many ASTD chapters throughout the United States.

Dr. Newstrom has written ten articles for the *Training and Development Journal,* serves on the Editorial Review Board for the *Journal of Management Development,* and is the co-author (with Ed Scannell) of the widely acclaimed books *Games Trainers Play, More Games Trainers Play, Still More Games Trainers Play,* and *Even More Games Trainers Play.* He has also co-authored, in recent years:

- *The Manager's Bookshelf* (with Jon Pierce)
- *Organizational Behavior* (with Keith Davis)
- *Windows into Organizations* (with Jon Pierce)
- *What Every Supervisor Should Know* (with Lester Bittel)
- *Transfer of Training* (with Mary Broad)
- *Leaders and the Leadership Process* (with Jon Pierce)